SKILLED TRADE PROFESSIONALS

T0312672

PRACTICAL CAREER GUIDES

Series Editor: Kezia Endsley

Dental Assistants and Hygienists, by Kezia Endsley
Education Professionals, by Kezia Endsley
Health and Fitness Professionals, by Kezia Endsley
Medical Office Professionals, by Marcia Santore
Skilled Trade Professionals, by Corbin Collins

SKILLED TRADE PROFESSIONALS

A Practical Career Guide

CORBIN COLLINS

ROWMAN & LITTLEFIELD
Lanham • Boulder • New York • London

Published by Rowman & Littlefield
An imprint of The Rowman & Littlefield Publishing Group, Inc.
4501 Forbes Boulevard, Suite 200, Lanham, Maryland 20706
www.rowman.com

6 Tinworth Street, London, SE11 5AL, United Kingdom

British Library Cataloguing in Publication Information Available

Library of Congress Cataloging-in-Publication Data

Names: Collins, Corbin, author.
Title: Skilled trade professionals : a practical career guide / Corbin Collins.
Description: Lanham, MD : Rowman & Littlefield Publishing Group, Inc., [2019] |
    Series: Practical career guides | Includes bibliographical references.
Identifiers: LCCN 2018058282 (print) | LCCN 2019011488 (ebook) |
    ISBN 9781538111802 (electronic) | ISBN 9781538111796 (pbk. : alk. paper)
Subjects: LCSH: Vocational guidance. | Job hunting. | Commerce.
Classification: LCC HF5381 (ebook) | LCC HF5381 .C684295 2019 (print) |
    DDC 650.14—dc23
LC record available at https://lccn.loc.gov/2018058282

Contents

Introduction: So You Want a Career in the Skilled Trades?   vii

1 Why Choose a Career in the Skilled Trades?   1
2 Forming a Career Plan   25
3 Pursuing the Education Path   49
4 Writing Your Résumé and Interviewing   81

Glossary   105
Notes   109
Resources   113
Bibliography   117
About the Author   121

Introduction: So You Want a Career in the Skilled Trades?

*W*elcome to the skilled trades! You've come to the right book to find out more about these popular and fulfilling careers.

Lots of different kinds of jobs are available in the skilled trades—hundreds of them, in fact. The employment website Monster.com, for example, lists thirty-one categories under the broad term *skilled trades*.[1] These include a wide range of fields, including welding, firefighting, locksmithing, kitchen cabinet installation, crane operation, farm and oilfield work, and lots more. The US Bureau of Labor Statistics offers data on some fifty categories of jobs just within one category it calls "installation, maintenance, and repair occupations."[2]

A Career in the Skilled Trades

There's not nearly enough room in this book to cover all the kinds of jobs that fall under the category of skilled trades, so instead the focus here is on five of the more popular and widely available types of jobs:

- Electrician
- Heating, ventilation, and air conditioning (HVAC)[3] technician
- Plumber
- Construction worker
- Automotive service technician/mechanic

These jobs are widely available pretty much all over the country. They pay pretty well, too, considering they don't require a four-year college degree. And there are currently shortages of workers for these jobs, which means that right now there are more open positions available for these jobs than there are people applying for them. That's good news for anyone looking to enter one of these professions. The foreseeable future looks bright for these jobs as well, as you'll see.

The Market Today

How does the job market look for young people seeking to enter the skilled trades? Very good. Demand for workers in the skilled trades is high and likely to only increase in the foreseeable future. According to *Forbes* magazine, employers are finding it even harder to fill positions in the skilled trades than in the famously in-demand fields of nursing and web development.[4]

There are a couple of reasons why the demand for skilled trade professionals is likely to grow in the future. First, over the past few decades the emphasis in American education has been on preparing students to attend college or university in order to gain access to higher-paying jobs, rather than on steering students toward vocational schools (sometimes called technical schools or career colleges), where they learn the skills necessary for many jobs in the skilled trades. This emphasis on college academics over the years has led to fewer young people entering the skilled trades.

Second, the average age of workers currently in the skilled trades is older than it is for the working population as a whole. People in these professions also retire earlier than the average worker because jobs in the skilled trades tend to be very demanding in terms of the physical work required. Workers in the skilled trades often leave their careers earlier at a younger age because they can't keep up physically, which means that more workers leave the job market every year than is typical in most other fields. Combined, these factors have created a very strong demand for new workers in the skilled trades, and that doesn't seem likely to change anytime soon.

The current shortage of skilled trade professionals in the job market today combined with the likelihood that the demand will only increase means wages in the skilled trades are set to go up as well. After all, economics tells us that low supply and high demand in a job market puts upward pressure on wages because companies must pay more in order to find good workers, which are relatively scarce. Because of this, now is a very good time to consider beginning a career in the skilled trades.

> The best part of the job: "Instant gratification, being able to stand back at the end of the day/end of the project and see the progress you made."—Tom Moser, owner/operator of Moser's Painting

Construction equipment operators lay a 280-foot casing pipe to protect utility lines at Chicago's O'Hare International Airport. *Courtesy of Andrew Dixon*

What Does This Book Cover?

This book covers the following topics for each of the five selected trades:

- Why you might want to choose a career in a particular trade, including descriptions of what the job involves day in and day out
- How to form a career plan and how to go about getting yourself ready for employment in the field
- The typical educational requirements for each career, and how to achieve them
- How to write your résumé, do well in interviews, and apply for jobs
- Terminology and resources for further investigation

By the time you've finished this book, you should know quite a bit about the skilled trades and how to go out and get a job in one of these fields.

HEATING AND COOLING THE OLD-SCHOOL WAY

Eric Milburn.
Courtesy of Eric Milburn

Eric Milburn is a service manager at TL Myers HVAC in Frankfort, Indiana, where he has worked for twenty-two years. Here he's checking a twenty-ton chiller using ultraviolet (UV) dye added to the system. His UV flashlight will make the dye glow wherever there is a refrigerant leak.

What is a typical day on the job for you?

I don't know if there is such a thing as a typical day in heating and cooling. Every day is a new day to learn something new. Most days start off by getting my agenda—usually eight to ten calls. Depending on the season, these are either heating or cooling calls. Those calls may take six to eight hours to finish or ten to sixteen hours.

What's the best part of your job?

The best part is knowing I am helping people. I also like meeting new people and catching up with the yearly customers from season to season.

What's the worst or most challenging part of your job?

The worst part of my job has to be the weather. It's either blazing hot or freezing cold when we are at our busiest, and it is exhausting. And it takes a lot of time away from my family.

What's the most surprising thing about your job?

The most surprising thing is that there are quite a few people who don't realize their furnace has a filter—until I change it after ten years.

What's next? Where do you see yourself going from here?

I would like to take what I have learned in my overall twenty-nine years of HVAC life and work at a facility where I can still work inside and outside to help maintain that facility. Then, like most people, retire in a modest-climate area that is quiet.

Did your education prepare you for the job?

I would say growing up my curiosity helped the most, in my experience. I was always taking things apart or trying to make something broken work. I didn't go to the normal tech school. I got my start in HVAC the old-fashioned way—hands-on at the age of sixteen as a summertime job!

Is the job what you expected?

The work I do is more than what I expected, but that's what has made the job so interesting. The constant changing of equipment, and more efficient, different refrigerants. And how there are no two systems that are alike, even though they might have identical equipment.

═══════════

Where Do You Start?

Almost all of these jobs start with completing high school. At a minimum, employers want and expect you to have the basic knowledge that is provided by the nation's public schools. For many of these jobs you need a solid grounding in math, science, geometry, and English, along with what you can learn in machine shop and woodworking classes. Knowledge of chemistry, physics, algebra, and economics will also come in handy and can set you apart from other people seeking the same kind of work.

You should really think long and hard about what interests you and what you enjoy doing. If you're attracted to a job just because you heard it pays a lot of money but you actually hate the day-to-day work the job entails, you will quickly find yourself frustrated and unhappy in your work. That's a bad place to be. It's much better in the long run to find something you like to do or that you find interesting and then form a career plan that allows you to do that. This book will help you become familiar with five different types of jobs in the skilled trades—but remember, as mentioned earlier, there are many, many more.

After high school, the usual path involves enrolling in a vocational school program in your chosen trade, applying to become an apprentice in a position that offers on-the-job training, or both. The information in chapter 3 covers that bit of the path.

Right now, though, the way to start is by turning the page!

Why Choose a Career in the Skilled Trades?

College isn't for everybody. Not everyone wants to—or can afford to—spend four or more years at a university taking academic classes in order to qualify for a "good job." Many good jobs have been overlooked for decades by the educational system, which chose to focus on preparing students for college. As for young people who do go to college, four out of ten end up dropping out without a degree, many of them heavily burdened by large school loans.

So what else is there? Are there any jobs that pay pretty well that don't require a university education? Yes. The skilled trades, sometimes called the vocational trades, include work in many different fields across almost all sectors of the economy. There are lots and lots of these skilled trades—carpenters, drillers, roofers, crane operators—far too many to list here. This book focuses on five of the more common skilled trades in the electrical, HVAC, plumbing, construction, and automotive repair and service fields.

This chapter introduces these five common skilled trades and discusses their pros and cons. It talks about how healthy the job market currently is in these industries, and what the prospects are for good jobs in the future. It also outlines the required skill sets and personality types needed to succeed in these careers, so that you can determine whether or not you would be a good fit.

The good news about these kinds of jobs is that just about *anything* to do with building things and keeping them running in the modern world requires the work of people in various skilled trades. This means a vocational path that starts in one of these areas can become a solid foundation for a lifelong career, even with the constant changes in today's technologies and job markets. For example, nobody even knows what kinds of technologies automotive mechanics and HVAC technicians will need to know about in twenty years—but we do know that we will need people to learn, install, maintain, and repair those technologies.

And there's more good news. Jobs in the skilled trades can be found in almost every town and city in the United States. These are all careers that can, in many circumstances, offer room to advance up the management ladder, too. Many people in the skilled trades strike out on their own, working independently for themselves or starting shops and companies of their own. The skilled trades also offer many opportunities to specialize.

Still more good news: These jobs tend to pay pretty well—enough in many cases to build a career, live in a nice place, and raise a family. For those with a lot of experience in a high-demand or specialized field, jobs in this sector pay even better. For example, according to the website Salary.com, the average annual pay for a journeyman electrician (you'll learn what a journeyman is later) in 2018 is $58,036.[1] But for an avionics electrician—one who works on the electrical systems of airplanes—average annual pay is $63,778.[2] (You'll find out in chapter 4 just how much a $5,000 or $6,000 difference in annual pay adds up over the years.) Some tradespeople end up owning their own businesses, while others work for small, medium, or large companies.

For some folks, maybe the best news of all is that most work in the skilled trades doesn't require a college education. However, you *do* need to finish high school, and most jobs in the skilled trades require vocational or technical education and training, which may last anywhere from six months to two years. This specialized, focused schooling, designed to prepare you to become certified to work in a particular skilled trade, usually takes place at local vocational schools, trade schools, and community colleges, and involves a fair bit of science and math coursework. (One exception to this is construction laborer, a job that may not even require a high school diploma; however, this job pays less than the other skilled trades discussed here, and if you want to advance in construction, you'll need some schooling.)

The other main way of training for one of these jobs is through on-the-job training. In this method, you are hired by a company at a beginning wage, and your job is to accompany, watch, and learn from an employee who has experience in that particular job. Some skilled trades require both vocational and on-the-job training.

In some skilled trades, including the electrical, HVAC, and automotive service fields, staying up-to-date on changing technology has become a fact of life. New and upgraded systems keep appearing year after year, some of them revolutionary in nature. Remaining competitive in these fields means your education doesn't stop at certification or when you get your first job. In fact, in a sense, it never really stops.

What Are the Skilled Trades?

The skilled trades encompass a huge variety of jobs usually involving the installation, servicing, maintenance, and repair of physical equipment and systems. The term may be applied to many different sectors of the economy. The trades discussed in this book fall into categories often called industrial, manufacturing, construction, repair, and maintenance, though these categories aren't always firm.

Within each category you'll find dozens of different types of jobs, including different levels according to experience. Some are jobs you start out in as a beginner (called apprentice jobs, in many cases), some jobs are available for those who have a few years' experience (often called journeyman jobs), and some jobs are available for those with lots of experience (the master level). Companies that hire people in the skilled trades also need managers to supervise workers and guide their careers, to negotiate contracts, and to plan, hire, and budget for projects. If you can see yourself in that role one day, find out how managers in your field are hired and what additional education you may need, and set this as a goal.

There is also a great deal of specialization within each job category. An electrician, for example, might specialize in repairing and maintaining electrical systems in residential homes and local businesses or on building new electrical systems on-site for new construction projects. Other electricians work on larger integrated power systems, such as those found in factories, airports, and college and hospital campuses. Still other electricians specialize in the particular electrical systems that run elevators, utility company equipment, subway trains, cargo ships, or various types of industrial machinery—to name just a few options.

These jobs can vary according to which company you choose to work for, or whether you want to work for yourself. Plumbers might start their own plumbing service businesses, put their name on a truck loaded with tools and pipes, and start advertising. Or they might work for a small or medium-sized business that provides plumbing service to residential homes, or to homes and businesses, or to large industrial concerns. Some plumbers work for construction companies, installing entire plumbing and drainage systems in new buildings. Some work for municipalities, cities, or states, performing safety and compliance inspections. And some work for power companies and utilities, maintaining public water and sewer lines.

Working in the skilled trades can be physically demanding and may involve long hours, weekend work, and overtime. Working conditions aren't always comfortable or clean. You may find yourself trying to get necessary work done in cramped, dark, wet, hot, or cold environments. Some work—especially in the electrical and construction fields—can be quite dangerous.

UNION DECLINE AND SHRINKING NON-COLLEGE OPTIONS

For much of the twentieth century, there were many industrial career paths to the middle class that didn't involve earning a degree. Jobs in factories, manufacturing, mining, transportation, and many similar fields often paid well enough for an individual to live a comfortable life, raise a family in a nice home, and generally enjoy the fruits of the American dream. It was unions that made much of that possible. In a union, an organized labor team represents the workers in collective bargaining with management to negotiate the fair distribution of the profits earned by the big industrial companies.

Slowly that arrangement began to weaken, and it has continued to weaken. Government began stepping back from promoting unions, and the relative power of corporations began to rise. Courts started chipping away at union rights and powers. Union membership began to decline, which meant the bargaining power of workers also declined, so the wages paid to workers stopped growing as quickly as they once did. The trend has continued into the twenty-first century. As late as 1983, union membership in the United States stood at 20.1 percent, with 17.7 million union workers. Today those figures are 10.7 percent union membership and 14.8 million union workers.[3]

But unions aren't gone. Some skilled trade jobs today still involve union membership. Unions often sponsor apprenticeships, which offer a combination of classroom instruction and on-the-job training.

ELECTRICIAN

An electrician is responsible for installing, maintaining, or repairing the electrical wiring in the power systems of buildings or equipment. Some electricians, called voice-data-video (VDV) electricians, work only on low-voltage systems.

The three levels of electrician are apprentice, journeyman, and master electrician:

- Apprentice electricians are those just starting out. An apprentice electrician must take a minimum number of hours of coursework, typically at a community or technical college. An apprentice is assigned a journeyman as a mentor. Apprentices work with their mentors, learning the trade as they go while being paid less than a journey-level salary. Apprenticeship typically lasts two to six years. Apprentices cannot work unsupervised.
- Journeyman electricians have gone through apprenticeship and met the electrician licensing requirements of their local governing authorities. Journey-level electricians may do work unsupervised, though all work must be done under the authority and direction of a master electrician.

An electrician working at a home construction site.

- Master electricians have succeeded in the journeyman role for seven to ten years. They have also demonstrated knowledge of the National Electrical Code (NEC), which is the standard for the safe installation of electrical wiring in the United States, by passing an exam. Master electricians work unsupervised.

Electrician apprenticeship training is often sponsored by unions and by companies and associations of companies that hire electricians.

The focus of the work of electricians is generally divided into linemen, who work on power lines and other outdoor electrical distribution systems maintained by power companies, and wiremen, who work mostly on the wiring inside buildings. Because of the dangers inherent in electricity, strict regulations and standards govern who can work on electrical systems. Licensing requirements for electricians vary from state to state.

Almost any situation that involves electricity will at some point require the services of an electrician. Electricians may work for small or large employers, including building contractors, consumer and business service companies, governments, large public building complexes such as hotels and universities, and public utilities. Or they may work for themselves and contract with various clients and customers as needed.

HVAC TECHNICIAN

HVAC stands for heating, ventilation, and air conditioning. HVAC technicians work on heating and cooling units, such as air-conditioning and furnace heating systems, as well as air circulation systems in buildings of all types. Sometimes they work on refrigeration systems, too.

It is the job of HVAC technicians to ensure proper temperature control and air quality. The air in buildings must continually circulate to the outside to remove pollutants, moisture, smoke, and any other harmful gases that can build up in enclosed spaces, and HVAC technicians work on the systems that circulate, heat, and cool the air.

HVAC technicians often begin their training in a community or technical college, learning applicable fundamentals of physics and math as they relate to HVAC principles. There are apprenticeship opportunities for HVAC and union trade programs that can result in on-the-job training with companies. The training often involves attending classes in the evenings and working with

HVAC technicians working on an air conditioner.

experienced journeymen on jobs during the day. Apprenticeship details vary, but may last four years, at the end of which you can become a licensed journeyman HVAC technician and may work on HVAC systems unsupervised.

After a few years as a journeyman (the number of years varies from state to state), you may apply for a master's license, which will lead to—among other things—higher pay. A master's license is also required if you want to strike out on your own and start your own company working as an independent technician.

Employers of HVAC technicians include heating and cooling installation services, construction contractors, HVAC equipment manufacturers, and organizations that own or operate large building complexes, such as governments, hospitals, hotels, schools, and universities.

HVAC work can involve long hours, weekend work, and overtime. It can be demanding, strenuous, and at times uncomfortable—after all, no one would call you to come fix a heating or cooling system if it were working properly. Depending on your location, summer daytime hours may be spent in stuffy homes and businesses with broken AC units, and in the winter months nonfunctioning furnaces can make for some chilly work—until you fix things, that is.

HVAC technicians must stay up-to-date on the continually evolving technologies of heating, cooling, refrigeration, and air ventilation systems. It is important for HVAC technicians to keep up with increasingly complex and powerful equipment technology and stay knowledgeable about regulations regarding environmentally proper refrigerant elements.

Moving from working on HVAC systems to designing and manufacturing them is another possible career path, one that requires at least a bachelor's degree in mechanical engineering and gaining a thorough understanding of thermodynamics.

PLUMBER

Plumbers are tradespeople who install, maintain, and repair water piping systems. These may include public, business, and residential building plumbing systems; sewer systems; and drainage systems. Ensuring the continual and safe delivery of clean water is an essential part of modern life.

A plumber working on pipes under a kitchen sink.

As with many trades, becoming a plumber usually involves an apprenticeship in which you learn on the job with an experienced journeyman plumber for a number of years before earning the right to work independently. Formal training in a school setting may or may not be required, but if so it might not be as much as for the electrician and HVAC technician career paths.

As with electricians, those starting out in plumbing are known as apprentices, who learn from watching and helping journeyman plumbers. Journeyman plumbers have several years of experience and can do work on their own. A plumber with many years of experience can become a master, often by taking a state exam. Some states require that plumbing businesses employ at least one master plumber in order to obtain a plumbing contractor's license.

Plumbers with enough experience can work for themselves, and many work for plumbing service companies that employ several plumbers. These companies receive service calls and send their plumbers out to service residential and business customers in need of plumbing services. Large complexes such as government and other public buildings, universities, schools, factories, airports, train stations, and hospitals also employ plumbers to maintain and repair their water, sewage, and drainage systems.

Plumbers are often asked to work overtime and weekends. Plumbing itself can be difficult, messy work. A certain amount of physical strength and a good knowledge of the proper use of various tools are required due to the nature and locations of piping systems.

CONSTRUCTION LABORER, CRAFTSPERSON, AND MANAGER

Construction jobs involve erecting buildings and other large residential, commercial, industrial, and public structures. Construction work is done by crews usually made up of laborers, craftspeople, and supervisors.

- Laborers often perform the lifting, loading, hauling, and cleanup of building materials and assist the craftspeople on-site in other ways.
- Craftspeople are skilled specialists such as painters, carpenters, masons, crane and other machine operators, drillers, welders, and others who are responsible for completing certain segments of construction projects.
- Managers oversee budgets and/or organize and direct others on construction crews. These may include planners, foremen, supervisors, project managers, and other management roles.

Construction workers on scaffolding at a construction site.

There are few education requirements for laborers and craftspeople—less than in the other skilled trades covered in this book. Still, a high school degree and proficiency in English and math will open up many more opportunities in this industry. Vocational and trade schools offer training in areas like carpentry, masonry, and welding that can help speed up a career, but many craftspeople learn on the job through apprenticeships and similar arrangements. Construction management jobs usually require a bachelor's degree from a university, although promotion through the ranks to some supervisory positions is fairly common.

Depending on the project, work on construction sites can be rigorous and sometimes dangerous, as you might imagine. Work is usually paid hourly. Craftspeople earn higher wages than laborers, and managers earn higher wages than craftspeople.

AUTOMOTIVE SERVICE TECHNICIAN/MECHANIC

Jobs in the automotive repair and maintenance field involve repairing cars and other vehicles and keeping them running well. Mechanics and automotive

A professional mechanic repairing a car in an auto repair shop.

service techs usually work in garages. They must be skilled in the use of a wide variety of tools, including power tools. They must be good at problem solving, because much of the work consists of attempting to discover the source of mechanical trouble. And they must be comfortable using technology, including the advanced electronics and computer systems found in newer vehicles.

You might think of a mechanic as someone who knows how to fix automobile engines, but some service techs specialize in body work, which involves painting and repairing cosmetic damage to the outer surface of vehicles. Some specialize in glass replacement, fixing broken vehicle windshields and windows. Others become adept at repairing special vehicles, such as motorcycles or buses. Mechanics may find work at automobile dealerships or private repair garages, or with organizations that need mechanics to service their fleets of cars, such as police departments, car rental companies, and government and municipal agencies.

Many young people enjoy working on cars in their spare time and on weekends with friends. If this is you, consider whether you might want to do it full-time, or even overtime, every day. Entering the automotive service field requires obtaining certification after completing a program at a technical or vocational school. Because of the rapidly changing and increasingly complex technologies built into today's cars, certifications must be regularly refreshed with continued study and updated coursework. It used to be that a high school diploma was enough to get your foot in the door at a garage, but these days employers are looking for graduates of quality programs that teach updated technology.

Pay is somewhat lower in automotive service than in some of the other trade careers, especially to start with. But your income also depends on how much you want to work. If you log a lot of hours, including overtime, at a popular, well-respected garage, wages can be decent.

The Pros and Cons of Skilled Trade Careers

Assessing the pros and cons of trade careers is hard to do in general because there is such variation in work environment and in the skills and schooling required, even among the five areas this book focuses on. Here are a few generally positive things these jobs often have in common:

- *Variation:* These jobs involve working on-site at locations that may change from project to project.
- *Hands-on work:* These jobs require solving problems, working repairs, maintaining and operating machines, and building things with your hands.
- *Physical work:* Many of these jobs involve physical effort.
- *Outdoor work:* These are not desk or office jobs. Tradespeople, even managers, spend more time outside and in open areas.
- *Portability:* If you have some experience, you should have little trouble finding work wherever you choose to live in the United States.
- *Working directly with others:* A trade career often involves working among your customers (electrician, plumber, HVAC tech) or coworkers (construction, automotive).
- *Pretty good pay:* Considering the savings achieved by not paying for a full four-year university education, these jobs usually pay a decent wage.

Some of the not-so-positive aspects of working in trade careers include:

- *Physical exhaustion:* These jobs often involve lifting, hauling, and performing other demanding physical labor that can take a toll on the body, which can, in turn, lead to injuries. Workers in the trade careers tend to leave the workforce at an earlier age than those who stand at counters or sit at computers all day.

- *Exposure to weather:* Just because it's raining doesn't mean you're getting the day off. You may have to wear special clothing and put up with freezing temperatures; hot, stuffy attics; or cold, flooded basements.
- *Keeping up with technology:* Because these jobs often involve working with machinery and other technology, the relentless pace of innovation and constant improvements often mean you can never decide that you've learned enough. Next year, there will be a new technology you'll have to study and figure out, and you may have to take a class for that.
- *Working evenings and weekends:* Things tend to go wrong outside the hours between nine and five. Many jobs in the trade careers involve weekend and evening work, and sometimes even holidays. If you are a plumber or electrician and get an emergency call, you'll have to suit up and head out to the site to fix whatever has happened, no matter the time of day.

Your own preferences count most of all when it comes time to consider the good and not-so-good aspects of anything, especially a career. Take some time and think about what you truly enjoy doing—and what you find boring, tedious, or frustrating.

BUT AREN'T THE ROBOTS GOING TO TAKE ALL THE JOBS?

We hear a lot today about automation in the workplace. It is true that in recent years many jobs have been replaced by robots and other automated systems. Automation makes it cheaper for machines to do certain jobs. For example, in many factories today, robots and other machinery are doing jobs that used to belong to humans. In many supermarkets and superstores, machines do the job that checkout clerks used to do—or, more exactly, machines help *you* do the checkout job. The machine reads the price of the items you pass in front of the scanner, tallies them all up, and accepts your payment. The job of bagging your items falls entirely to you.

Modern automation often involves artificial intelligence (AI), which replaces human analysis and decision making. AI is already well established in the business world, especially in the worlds of finance and stock trading. In the future, it is supposed that AI will prove better than humans at many tasks, including reading X-rays and MRI scans and diagnosing diseases. If even doctors' jobs aren't safe, does this mean jobs in the skilled trades are soon to be history as well?

Probably not anytime soon. For one thing, historically, when certain jobs become obsolete, other jobs appear to take their place. If your job in 1905 was making buggy whips, then yes, your job was soon going away forever—but then again, you might get a job at the new automobile factory opening across town. In one study of 800,000 jobs lost to automation, it was found that 3.5 million jobs were created. As business writer Daniel Browning puts it, "Although it is difficult to predict exactly what jobs the future of automation will create, the ability to maintain and operate machines is one still wholly relegated to people."[4] It's reasonable to think that the number of skilled trade jobs may actually *grow* in spite of automation. After all, if the robots do come and take lots more jobs, who's going to install, upgrade, maintain, service, fix, and replace them when things go wrong? People in the skilled trades, that's who.

How Healthy Is the Job Market for Skilled Trade Careers?

As noted earlier in the introduction, the job market for skilled trade careers is currently strong and seems likely to continue that way into the future. In fact, many of these occupations are experiencing shortages in workers, which means more job opportunities—and usually higher pay. The following sections look at the job market for each of the five skilled trade careers explored in this book.

Note that the wage numbers given in the following subsections refer to median wage, which means half of the people in the occupation earn less, and half earn more. The statistics used come from the US Bureau of Labor Statistics (www.bls.gov) and include data as of the end of 2017.

ELECTRICIAN

Because construction continues to be strong in the economy, there is a high demand for electricians to wire up all the new building projects. The Bureau of

Labor Statistics projects the job market for electricians will grow by 9 percent between 2016 and 2026,[5] which is slightly faster than the projected growth for all occupations. So the future for electricians is as bright or brighter than the future for all American workers.

Areas of specialization for electricians that are likely to grow in the future include alternative power sources such as wind and solar. These new plants and systems will need more electricians as they expand. If given the opportunity to work on alternative power, you should consider it seriously. Its growth and success, however, may depend on how it is viewed by different governments that come into power.

- *Hourly pay:* $26.01
- *Annual wage:* $54,110
- *Projected growth (2016–2026):* 9 percent (faster than average)[6]

Alternative power represents a new career path emerging for electricians.

HVAC TECHNICIAN

Like the job prospects for electricians, the outlook for HVAC technicians depends to a large extent on the health of the construction industry. Currently, that means prospects are good. New buildings need new heating, ventilation, and air-conditioning systems, which means HVAC workers are needed to install them. The Bureau of Labor Statistics projects very fast job growth in the HVAC field—more than twice the growth projection for all jobs.

Besides installing new systems, HVAC techs spend a lot of time repairing and maintaining systems that are already installed, and they also spend time upgrading and retrofitting existing systems as new technologies become available. In this field, improvements in energy efficiency and revisions to environmental regulations often lead to rapid technological change in HVAC equipment. HVAC techs must stay abreast of such changes and be ready to bring old systems up to new standards or replace them with new equipment models.

- *Hourly pay:* $22.64
- *Annual wage:* $47,080
- *Projected growth (2016–2026):* 15 percent (much faster than average)[7]

PLUMBING

As with the other careers so far, plumbing involves both installing new systems and repairing and maintaining older systems. Construction contractors need plumbers to install new water, sewer, and drainage systems on building projects, so the fortunes of plumbing in general go up and down with the fortunes of construction.

However, even during recessions, people and businesses need their existing systems to work, so there is always plumbing work to do. And it turns out there is a lot of it, with a lot more on the way. The Bureau of Labor Statistics projects job growth for plumbing will be a blistering 16 percent between 2016 and 2026. That is more than twice as fast as the average growth anticipated for all jobs. Clearly, plumbing has a bright future, at least for the next ten years.

Similar to plumbing are the jobs of steamfitter, pipefitter, and sprinklerfitter. Where plumbers install and repair pipes that carry water, steamfitters and pipefitters work on pipes that carry all kinds of things, including highly pressurized steams and gases. Sprinklerfitters work on modern fire suppression systems built into all new construction. These jobs are projected to grow as rapidly as plumbing.

- *Hourly pay:* $25.38
- *Annual wage:* $52,590
- *Projected growth (2016–2026):* 16 percent (much faster than average)[8]

CONSTRUCTION

A large portion of the construction industry involves the erection of new buildings. Historically, the health of the construction industry follows the health of the economy as a whole. When the economy is doing well, people and businesses have more money to invest in new buildings. When the economy is slowing or shrinking, construction takes a painful hit.

For example, if wages are improving, more people will be willing to start the process of buying a house, which means more houses will need to be built, which means more people will be needed to work in residential housing construction. If corporate profits are up, many businesses will spend money to

Construction involves a variety of activity and work—never a dull moment!

expand so they can make more money, which means more commercial real estate development will take place—and more hiring in construction to get that done. If a state finds itself with a surplus of money in a certain year, it may choose to finally fix those crumbling roads, sidewalks, bridges, and buildings, hiring lots of construction workers to do it.

As of late 2018, the number of construction jobs available in the United States has been growing since 2010. There are around a quarter of a million job openings in construction across the country. The Bureau of Labor Statistics projects faster-than-average employment growth in construction through 2026.

Pay rates in construction vary by quite a bit, with laborers and helpers earning the least and managers earning the most. In between are the craftspeople such as carpenters and equipment operators, who earn somewhere in the middle.

Laborers and Helpers

Laborers and helpers do physical work on construction sites, such as cleaning, hauling, digging, building, tearing down, and removing construction debris. They also assist other workers, including craftspeople and managers, on the site.

- *Hourly pay:* $16.08
- *Annual wage:* $33,450
- *Projected growth (2016–2026):* 12 percent (faster than average)[9]

Craftspeople

Dozens of different jobs fall into the broad "craftsman" category. Often these are somewhat specialized jobs requiring dedicated training. Equipment operator is a typical example. These workers drive and operate heavy machinery such as bulldozers, backhoes, excavators, and graders used in building large structures.

- *Hourly pay:* $22.15
- *Annual wage:* $46,080
- *Projected growth (2016–2026):* 12 percent (faster than average)[10]

Managers

Managers supervise other employees and work on planning, scheduling, and budgeting for entire construction projects.

- *Hourly pay:* $43.93
- *Annual wage:* $91,370
- *Projected growth (2016–2026):* 11 percent (faster than average)[11]

What goes up must come down! Economies can and do take occasional downturns. It's just a fact of life, even if you haven't experienced it yet. When—not if—the economy stalls or goes into reverse, construction is one of the first sectors to be hit. The project your company was going to get next week may suddenly be canceled. In the construction industry, you have to take the bad with the good and be prepared to weather the tough times, which can include periods of unemployment.

AUTOMOTIVE SERVICE AND MAINTENANCE

Job prospects for automotive service technicians and mechanics are fairly good and likely to remain so. The Bureau of Labor Statistics projects 6 percent growth in jobs in this field from 2016 to 2026, about the same as the average for all jobs in the country. The number of vehicles on the road keeps going up, and that alone should create demand for auto techs and mechanics.

Even more than in HVAC, automotive technology is constantly changing and improving. Modern cars have highly sophisticated systems incorporating computers. Service techs and mechanics of the future will need to be able to keep up with these changes. An even bigger change—the arrival of driverless vehicles—is already on the horizon. As far back as 2010, Google had been secretly testing driverless cars in real traffic situations. These new cars will also need repair and maintenance and are likely to present entirely new technologies for auto service techs and mechanics to learn. This development will likely drive the future automotive repair job market.

Pay in this field is a bit lower than in some of the other trade careers. However, the ever-increasing technological complexity and the coming wave of driverless cars is likely to increase the value of repair work, which in turn should raise wages somewhat.

- *Hourly pay:* $19.02
- *Annual wage:* $39,550
- *Projected growth (2016–2026):* 6 percent (about average)[12]

Am I Right for a Skilled Trade Career?

The answer to this question depends not just on your particular skill set and personality, but on your preferences regarding how you like to work, what you like to work on, and what you find interesting about how you spend your time. Equally, you need to consider what you *don't* like to spend your time doing. The two main attributes that can affect your success in a chosen career are skill set and personality. Skill set refers to the abilities you have acquired in terms of accomplishing different tasks, and personality, of course, refers to more general things about you such as outlook, mood, energy level, level of optimism, whether you tend to be outgoing or introverted, and other aspects of your behavior.

Generally, people who succeed in the skilled trades tend to be:

- Physically healthy and strong
- Friendly to coworkers and customers
- Curious of mind and able to figure out gadgets
- Good at spotting sources of trouble and determining what may be going wrong with a system
- Able to use math and geometry to quickly assess the kinds and sizes of materials needed for a project
- Adept at using tools, including power tools

And let's be honest. Not everyone is cut out for advanced academic schooling that goes on for four or more years. Some people become bored or anxious when forced to learn subjects they have no interest in. Some can't easily concentrate on reading (this book being an exception, of course!) or listening to lectures for long periods. Some try and try but find they just don't seem to have the aptitude for school. If that's you, or if you can relate to those descriptions, the skilled trades can offer a good choice of career.

One way to see whether you may be cut out for a career in the skilled trades is to ask yourself the following questions:

- *Would I prefer to be active and moving around during work, or would I rather mostly stay put behind a desk?*

  People who work in the skilled trades are definitely up and moving about more than people who work in an office. If the thought of being on your feet all day lifting and pushing and pulling and carrying things sounds all right, then you're physically well suited to most of this work.

- *When something breaks, am I the type who wants to figure out how to fix it, or do I immediately ask someone else to do that?*

  These types of jobs seem to attract tinkerers and people who like to take things into their own hands to fix or figure out. That's not to say you need to be that way, but it will help, because confronting technical problems and getting stuff to work correctly are all in a day's work in many of these jobs.

- *When I'm under someone's supervision and they tell me to do something, do I immediately do it or do I question and resist, or claim I know a better way?*

  Although independent thought and self-direction are good (see chapter 4 for more on this), you need to be able to follow direction from authority, especially when you are starting out. That's not just because organizations run more smoothly when workers do what they're asked to do—and this is true, of course—it's also because many of these jobs involve using machinery and tools in environments that can be dangerous. People with experience have seen the problems that can arise and have already figured out good ways to do the job while staying safe. You may indeed see a better way—and if so, you should feel free to speak up—but it's best to learn the existing rules thoroughly before breaking or trying to change them.

- *Can I see myself owning my own business one day?*

  After learning the trade from those who have more experience, plenty of electricians, plumbers, HVAC techs, auto mechanics, and construction workers strike out on their own, setting up their own businesses, garages, and shops. That's a good thing. If you can see yourself keeping the books and hiring other people someday, starting your own business may be a goal as you move into your career. Then again, if you see yourself working for a company or series of companies for your whole career, that's completely fine, too. That's what most people do.

- *Can I consistently deal with people in a professional, friendly way?*
Many jobs in the skilled trades will have you working closely with fellow employees, following orders from one or more bosses, and/or dealing directly with customers (sometimes in their homes) who may not be in the best mood. Being able to handle interpersonal relations in a professional manner is very important to a career in many skilled trades. It can directly impact how much business your company gets through word-of-mouth recommendations, for example, which affects how much money you can be paid. Who do you think would get a better recommendation from a customer: an electrician who shows up late, mumbles answers to questions, complains about the temperature or the working conditions or his boss, and fixes a fuse box—or one who arrives on time, makes polite conversation, answers questions in a friendly manner, explains what he's doing, and fixes a fuse box?

The answers to these questions can provide some insight into you, your skill set, and your personality, but sometimes we're not sure about ourselves, especially at a young age. Another good way to figure out whether a skilled trades career might be right for you is to ask other people, especially older people. Consider asking family, friends, teachers, and counselors what they think. Request that they be honest. You may be surprised at what they see that you didn't know about yourself.

KEEPING UP WITH AUTOMOTIVE TECHNOLOGY

Blaine Meyer.
Courtesy of Blaine Meyer

Blaine Meyer is owner/operator of Confident Auto Repair in Indianapolis, Indiana. He started his own business after ten years working in his trade.

What is a typical day on the job for you?

I start the day by checking my schedule and then begin bringing in the cars and diagnosing them. When I know what's wrong and what I need to do to fix it, I start calling around for parts and prices. Then I call the customers and let them know those prices. If they accept the work, I fix their vehicle and then repeat these steps until the end of the day.

What's the best part of your job?

My favorite part of the job is diagnosing problems that nobody else can figure out. I also love to help my customers with great repairs at a fair price. Most people don't know anything about their cars, so I've found that being honest works well. It keeps me busy!

What's the worst or most challenging part of your job?

Sometimes I get very dirty—not the best thing in the world. But it happens. Also, sometimes I have to do a job twice due to defective parts, which kills my time management. It means I get backed up, and people still want their repairs done in a timely manner.

What's the most surprising thing about your job?

The surprises never stop. Manufacturers continue to do very complex technical changes that make working on autos hard. It's difficult to stay updated as things change. Who would have ever thought they would put air-conditioned steering wheels on cars?

What's next? Where do you see yourself going from here?

Well, I've been a tech since 1987, so about thirty years, and I've seen a lot of change. Twenty years ago I started my auto shop, and three years ago I was able to purchase the building I work in, so all in all I will be a business owner, auto tech, and building owner until I retire.

Did your education prepare you for the job?

Yes it did, although I wish I had studied harder in high school. All the things you learn there are wrapped into cars—math, chemistry, English, social studies, and so on. I also attended Lincoln College of Technology in Indianapolis for automotive training, which focused on theory.

Is the job what you expected?

I thought I knew what to expect, but I had no idea of the technical improvements that would happen on these cars year after year. They have become computer systems, which I have very little background in.

Summary

In this chapter, you learned a bit about five particular skilled trades: electrician, HVAC technician, plumber, construction worker, plumber, and automotive service technician/mechanic. You also learned that the skilled trades can be a reliably good career path for young people because they are an important, fundamental part of the economy.

You explored some of the pros and cons of starting a career in these five skilled trades. And you found out quite a bit about what these jobs are and what kind of work each one typically involves. You discovered that the job market for most skilled trades looks to be very bright for the foreseeable future. Even though automation is on the rise, threatening to replace jobs people do now with robots and AI systems, the skilled trades look to be fairly safe for now. Robots are not likely to be fixing sinks, replacing the wiring in restaurants, repairing broken steering wheels, or installing home furnace fans in basements anytime soon—these tasks still require the human touch. Machines still need humans to keep them operating in good condition, at least for now.

You read about the importance of knowing your skill set and personality in choosing a career path and about the types of skills and personality traits that often lead to success in the skilled trades. You learned some questions you can ask yourself (or friends and family) to help you determine whether this career path would be a good fit. And you met an auto mechanic who worked on cars for ten years before opening his own repair garage.

In the next chapter, you'll begin to focus on creating a career plan aimed at helping you pursue skilled trade jobs after high school.

Forming a Career Plan

You've probably heard the saying, "Failing to plan is planning to fail." And you've more than likely learned—maybe the hard way—the importance of planning in high school; for example, if you have an eight-page paper due in two weeks, you know the result will be better if you do some planning in order to make that deadline with plenty of time to spare. You need to choose and research the topic, then formulate a thesis (what you're going to argue), then write a general outline that hits the main points, then go back and start filling in the details with sentences and paragraphs, and so on. It's just in the nature of achieving complex goals that planning almost always helps.

This is especially true when it comes to planning a career. The problem here is that the goal is much bigger—in fact, it can seem so huge and intimidating that it becomes overwhelming, and you may end up not planning at all in order to avoid the whole thing. This is a normal reaction. But that's all it is—a reaction. If you must, go ahead and have that reaction. Let it come in and take over for a little while.

Feel better? Now come out of the fetal position and realize it doesn't actually have to be overwhelming. For one thing, you don't have to do it all at once; in fact, you couldn't. Do a little bit of career planning—then stop and do something else. Go shoot hoops, see a movie, or hang out with friends. Come back and do a little more career planning later. There's another saying that can come to your rescue here: "A path is laid one stone at a time."

This chapter covers these stones on your career-planning path, one at a time. It starts at the very beginning, with the first and easiest one: seeing what kind of job you might be good at and happy with. Then you'll look at some resources that can help you in your investigation into specific careers. After that, you'll learn how to go about making sure you direct your educational path and work experience toward these potential career goals so that when the time comes, you're prepared. The chapter finishes up by stressing the importance of using other people as a valuable resource—as you will see, people will probably turn out to be your most important career resource.

This chapter could just as well have been titled "How to Not End Up Miserable at Work"—because really, what all this is about is achieving happiness. After all, unless you're independently wealthy, you're going to have to work. That's just a given. If you work for eight hours a day, starting at age eighteen and retiring at age sixty-five, you're going to spend roughly a hundred thousand hours at work. That's about eleven years. Your life will be much, *much* better if you find a way to spend that time doing something you enjoy, that your personality is suited for, and that matches your particular skills and talents. Plenty of people don't get to do that, and you can often see it in their faces as you go about your day interacting with other people who are working. In all likelihood, they did not plan their careers very well and just fell into a random series of whatever jobs were available.

> The whole point of career planning is not to overwhelm you with a seemingly huge endeavor—it is to maximize happiness.

Planning the Plan

Maybe you already have some idea of what you want to do for a living, and presumably (because you're reading this book) it's one of the skilled trades. But maybe you have no idea, or just a vague idea. If you don't know what kind of work you want to do, keep reading. If you *do* have a pretty firm idea of what you want to do for a living, feel free to skip this section. But it may be a good idea to read it anyway, to make sure that what you want to do—or think you want to do—is a good fit for you.

At this beginning stage, it's usually helpful to start making lists. Lists are easy. You just sit and ask yourself questions and write down the answers. You don't have to use proper grammar or format them neatly or anything like that. Just grab a few pieces of paper or a notebook and pen. Or, if you're more comfortable, fire up your computer and start a new document. You can do this alone, or with a family member or a friend.

You're going to make three lists:

- Your personality traits
- Your skills
- Your interests

LIST 1: YOUR PERSONALITY TRAITS

Just sit and breathe for a minute or two and think about yourself. Pretend you're standing outside yourself, watching your life and the way you have developed and how it all has unfolded so far. Then ask yourself the following questions, one at a time, writing down everything that pops into your head:

1. What stands out about you? That is, what do people tend to notice about you right away?
2. What are you most proud of when you think about the way you deal with the world and other people?
3. Who are your heroes? Who would you like to become more like?

LIST 2: YOUR SKILLS

Next, think about how you've done at school and how things have worked out at any temporary or part-time jobs you've had so far, and answer the following questions:

1. What are you really good at, in your opinion? What have other people told you you're good at?
2. What are you not very good at right now, but you would like to become better at?
3. What are you not very good at, and you're okay with not getting better at?

LIST 3: YOUR INTERESTS

Now forget about work for a minute. In fact, forget about needing to ever have a job again. You won the lottery—congratulations! Now answer these questions:

1. What are your favorite three ways to spend your time?

2. For each of those things, can you describe why you think you in particular are attracted to it?
3. If you could get up tomorrow and do anything you wanted all day long, what would it be?

ASSESSING YOUR LISTS

Don't look at your lists right away. Put down your pen and go do something else. You've earned it. Let a day or more go by before you come back and look at what you wrote.

When you're ready, take out your list of personality traits and look it over. Pretend you're not you. Instead, you're a hiring manager at a company. What kind of job might be good for the person who wrote what you're reading? Does this person sound like someone who would work well with others? Do you think he or she would work better on their own, or helping out on a team? (For example, if you wrote down a sport as a favorite thing to do, was it something like tennis, swimming, or wrestling? If so, it may be that you prefer to achieve things more on your own, on your own terms. If you wrote down football, basketball, softball, or volleyball, it could be that you're more comfortable working together with others to achieve a common goal.)

What is this person good at? (Remember, you're looking at this as if you're looking to hire someone.) What does this person not seem to be good at? What does he or she want to improve on? Can you think of jobs where the skills he or she has would come in handy? Perhaps more importantly, can you think of jobs that don't fit this person's skills at all? What is this person interested in? If you hire this person, which jobs seem like they would keep this person somewhat interested and satisfied? What jobs would you steer him or her clear of?

How does this person like to spend time? What favorite activities have parallels in the workplace?

You're not expected to have a fully developed career goal after making these lists and looking them over. All of this is just a way of making sure you have some real idea of what you might or might not be suited for, what you might or might not be good at doing, and what you might or might not enjoy doing. You don't want to fool yourself, or aim too high or too low. You want to be in the ballpark of jobs that seem likely to make you feel good about how you're spending your days. After all, a career will (hopefully) last a long time. The better you fit yourself to the right kind of career, the happier your life will be.

But it's not always easy to be objective about yourself. Luckily, there are more detailed and systematic ways of assessing your suitability for different careers. These are covered in the next section.

Where to Go for Help

A number of resources are available to help you explore and narrow down your career choices. Here are some you may want to consider:

- For general information on jobs in the skilled trades, including median pay, education requirements, and how to get started in each trade, check out the Bureau of Labor Statistics Career Outlook site at www.bls.gov/careeroutlook.org. This site is a goldmine for all kinds of information on many different careers. You can search for whatever career you're interested in by typing it into the search box, or you can scroll through a list of career areas at www.bls.gov/careeroutlook/subject/home.htm.
- Have a look at the Explore the Trades website at https://explorethetrades .org. This site offers a wealth of information on the plumbing, HVAC, and electrical trades. You'll find links to career roadmaps, education resources, apprenticeships, training, and recruiting resources. While you're there, you can sign up for the site's mailing list.
- Check out the career test at Educations.com. Go to www.educations .com/career-test to take the thirty-five-question test. At the end, after you give your name, e-mail address, and country of residence, it will identify courses and careers that seem appropriate to you based on your test results.
- The Princeton Review website has a different online quiz at www.prince tonreview.com/quiz/career-quiz. It's twenty-four questions, each of which compares two professions, and you choose the one you would rather be in, assuming both pay the same salary. You see the results when you're done.
- Ask to talk to a high school guidance counselor about skilled trade careers. He or she will likely be able to offer you lots of information about local vocational schools, apprenticeships, and career opportunities.

- If you're still really confused and feel like you're no closer to knowing what you want to do, you may want to consult with a career coach or personal coach to help you refine your understanding of your goals and how to pursue them. These professionals specialize in figuring out what sorts of careers and jobs may be appropriate for different people.
- Interview people in your community who are working in jobs that you are considering. Feel free to ask them anything—what they enjoy about their work, what they find the most challenging, how they entered the field, advice on getting started, whether they would be willing to help you or provide a recommendation, and so on. You may even be able to visit them at their workplace and see firsthand what's involved. How do you find these people? Start asking around. You can ask your parents, your parents' friends, your teachers, and your school's guidance counselors. You could also search online using your hometown and the job title as keywords.
- Search online for local unions that represent workers in the kinds of jobs you're interested in. A good place to start is the Center for Union Facts (CUF) website at www.unionfacts.com/cuf. This is a comprehensive database of all kinds of facts about unions in America. The site offers easy ways to find different union organizations near you. Once you find a union near you, contact them to see if someone will talk to you about getting started in that profession. Many unions sponsor apprenticeship programs and other on-the-job training programs.

Making High School Count

A high school education is the foundation for a career in the skilled trades. Except for some construction laborer jobs, a high school education is required to pursue a career in any of the skilled trades, including electrician, HVAC technician, plumber, and automotive service technician.

You will almost certainly need more training beyond your high school courses, but high school is the best place to learn the basics of many skills that are put to use in the skilled trades. The following are some high school courses that can be of great benefit to anyone seeking work in the skilled trades:

- *Math:* You want to take as much math as you can, and at the highest level you can reasonably attain. Math teaches patience, logic, and discipline, and it trains your analytical and problem-solving skills. Those are all things you'll need in any of these careers. Jobs in the skilled trades typically require the use of math every day, especially for calculating fractions, decimals, percent, ratio, proportion, perimeter, area, and volume. From converting measurements to gathering the right amounts of materials, to using geometry and calculating angles, math is a subject you really can't know too much about.

- *English/language arts/communication:* The better you can communicate with others, the more efficient and effective you will be on the job. This is something employers truly value. And it's not just verbal skills that are important. Since so much of the work in the skilled trades involves operating and repairing machinery and equipment—often including new gadgets no one in the shop has ever seen before—an ability to quickly skim and understand technical manuals can set you up as someone who is quite valuable at work. Being able to communicate accurate complex technical information clearly to bosses, fellow employees, and customers is an important component of success in the skilled trades.

WHAT IF I DROPPED OUT OF HIGH SCHOOL?

In many ads for jobs, you'll see something like, "High school diploma or equivalent required." What does "equivalent" mean? It means you passed the General Educational Development (GED) exam. Once you earn that credential, you can use it like a high school diploma to pursue further technical or vocational (or college) education and to apply for jobs.

In most states you must be at least sixteen years old to take the GED exam, and in some states you must be eighteen. The exam covers four topic areas: math, language arts, science, and social studies. The GED exam is now administered only on computer, so you need to at least know how to work a mouse and keyboard. And you should be prepared to settle in, because completing the test usually takes all day.

You can register for the GED exam at www.ged.com. The website will also tell you everything you need to know about taking the exam, including when and where you can take it and any fees you'll need to pay.

- *Business/economics:* The goal of making money is what drives our economy and so it is also what drives the workplace. Understanding concepts like transactions, supply and demand, markets, profits, pricing, and tradeoffs can give you a leg up on fellow workers, who may struggle to understand the decisions or motivations of managers.

- *Science/physics/chemistry:* Science is a method of understanding the world through evidence and reason. Technology is really just applied science—building machines that let humans be more efficient and complete necessary tasks. Understanding science can help you quickly grasp the underlying principles behind machinery that you may be required to use, maintain, or repair. Chemistry and physics classes can be especially helpful in any number of ways down the line in any career in the skilled trades.

- *Social studies:* You may not see right away why studying history, government, or psychology would be necessary to fix a broken air conditioner. But the fact is, to get along smoothly in the modern workplace you need to know some background on your own culture and its institutions. Employers want their employees to be well-rounded and knowledgeable, and to be able to carry on conversations with other employees, managers, and customers. There are also many practical benefits. For example, psychology provides insights into why people do what they do and what their behavior says about them—you can rest assured that this comes in handy in the workplace. History tells us why things are the way they are and where these things came from. (For example, did you know the ancient Romans invented cement?) And of course the more you know about the government, the better you'll understand what it can and can't do to help or interfere with what you're trying to accomplish—not to mention how it can affect the business as a whole, your workplace environment, and your salary.

- *Vocational or shop classes:* Many high schools offer some kind of vocational classes as part of the school curriculum. Often called career and technical education, high school vocational courses can provide a head start in your career or in the additional education and training that will be necessary after high school. Courses often include automotive technology, building technology, drafting and mechanical design, business technology, and computer technology. Any and all of these will prove helpful as you embark on one of these careers.

Some vocational and trade schools offer courses for credit to qualifying high school students. Some even offer them in high schools. This is a great way to get some advanced technical training before you even graduate. Ask your guidance counselor whether your school offers trade school courses for credit.

Educational Requirements

Once you graduate high school (making sure you have taken the kinds of courses discussed in the previous section) or get your GED, then what? Well, it mostly depends on which career you're talking about. This section breaks down the educational requirements for all these career paths.

As you'll see, for most skilled trades, in-class education and hands-on training form a kind of joint path that leads into the work world. You'll likely need to take part in both kinds of learning, and in some ways they blend together. For example, most apprenticeship programs continue the same or similar classroom training you'll get in vocational school, and most vocational schools try to incorporate as much hands-on training into their courses as they can.

Here are some resources you can use to begin looking for vocational and technical schools. Most such schools offer a wide range of courses, which may include plumbing, HVAC, electrical, automotive technology, and construction science:

- *Federal Trade Commission (FTC): Choosing a Vocational School* (www .consumer.ftc.gov/articles/0241-choosing-vocational-school): This government site offers valuable advice and information about what to watch out for when exploring your vocational school options. Unfortunately, not all vocational schools are completely honest in the information they give prospective students. Here, the FTC suggests some warning signs to be alert to. You should do a lot of investigating into tuition and fees at whatever local vocational school you may be looking at. Check out all options for financial aid (more on that in the next chapter) and make sure you understand exactly how much it will cost to enroll in a program.

- *Trade Schools Guide* (www.trade-schools.net): Type your zip code into this website and it provides links to vocational schools near you, including online and on-campus programs. It also offers many helpful articles on attending trade school in general.
- *Accredited Schools Online* (www.accreditedschoolsonline.org/vocational -trade-school): This site lets you select what kind of degree or certificate you're interested in, a category, and a subject. It then returns links and recommendations based on your criteria. You have to provide your contact info in order to get details.
- *Home Builders Institute* (www.hbi.org): This organization offers apprenticeship programs for several skilled trades in many (though not all) places across the country. You can search for programs near you by entering your zip code.
- Your guidance counselor's office and your school or community library will have helpful information about nearby vocational schools.
- Sometimes the best place to begin is to enter search terms like "vocational technical schools skilled trades" and the name of your community into the search bar of your favorite search engine. This will provide lots of links to both local and online programs.

Online vocational training programs are becoming more and more common. In some cases, you can earn a diploma online in a little over a year, and they often cost significantly less than brick-and-mortar schools. Also, with an online program, the hours are more flexible and you can hold a job while you're completing the program. You can find online programs at the Trade Schools Guide and Accredited Schools Online links. Chapter 3 talks more about online vocational programs.

ELECTRICIAN

In all states, a high school diploma (or equivalent credential) is required in order to become an electrician. Usually, people become electricians by completing an on-the-job apprenticeship training program, but some electricians join the profession by completing a vocational or technical school electrician program and then finding a company that will hire them. Apprenticeships tend to prefer candidates who have some vocational training already. Some aspiring

An electrician instructor explaining tools to a student.

electricians enroll in vocational training courses while they look for an apprenticeship as a way to speed up their acceptance into an apprenticeship training program.

An apprenticeship is usually the most cost-effective way of getting into the field because apprentices are paid as they are undergoing the training (although they're paid much less than the journeyman electricians who train them)—in other words, you earn while you learn. Apprenticeships for electricians commonly last four or five years and involve approximately two thousand hours per year.[1] Many apprenticeships are sponsored by unions and associations of building contractors. Once the apprenticeship program has been completed, the apprentice becomes a journeyman and can work independently.

Vocational trade school programs emphasize concentrated courses in math, circuitry, wiring, safety, electrical theory, and electrical codes, along with supplemental skills like soldering and first aid. Often, one year in such a program is enough to earn acceptance into an apprenticeship. Many schools also offer an associate's degree in electrical technology that can be completed in as little as two years. Holding an associate's degree may pay off later in your career in terms of increased salary and speedier advancement.

Most states require electricians to pass an exam in order to become licensed to work, much of which covers the National Electrical Code (NEC). You'll need to find out about your local requirements by checking with your state's licensing board. Some states also require electricians to stay up-to-date on their training by continuing to take coursework in order to maintain their license.

HVAC TECHNICIAN

In all states, you'll find that a high school diploma (or equivalent credential) is required in order to become an HVAC technician. In most states, some kind of vocational education beyond high school is required as well. Some states and cities require HVAC technicians to be licensed, which involves passing a test.

Usually people become HVAC techs by completing an on-the-job apprenticeship training program after completing a certificate or associate's degree in an HVAC program at a vocational or community college. Common practice is to enroll in vocational training courses and then apply for an apprenticeship program. With an apprenticeship, you earn while you learn. Apprenticeships commonly last from three to five years, during which the apprentice is trained in using tools, working with cooling and heating systems, handling refrigerants, following safety regulations and practices, and many other tasks.

PLUMBER

A high school diploma (or equivalent credential) is normally required in order to become a plumber. Usually, people become plumbers by completing an on-the-job apprenticeship training program, but some plumbers join the profession by completing a vocational or technical school plumbing program and then finding a company that will hire them. You can enroll in vocational training courses while you look for an apprenticeship program.

Plumbing apprentices are paid as they undergo the training (although they're paid much less than the journeyman plumbers who train them)—in other words, you earn while you learn. Apprenticeships for plumbers commonly last four or five years, involving approximately two thousand hours per year.[2] Many apprenticeships are sponsored by unions and contracting associations. Once the apprenticeship program has been completed, the apprentice becomes a journeyman and can work independently.

Vocational trade school programs emphasize courses in tool use, pipe design, and safety. Plumbing codes and regulations, reading blueprints, and safety are also covered, along with mathematics, applied physics, and chemistry. Often, one year in such a program is enough to earn acceptance into an apprenticeship program. Many schools also offer an associate's degree in plumbing that can be completed in as little as two years. Holding an associate's degree may pay off later in your career in terms of increased salary and speedier advancement.

Most states require plumbers to have a certain amount of experience and to pass an exam in order to become licensed to work. This exam covers plumbing codes and trade practices. You'll need to find out about your local requirements by checking with your state's licensing board.

CONSTRUCTION LABORER, CRAFTSMAN, OR MANAGER

Construction laborer is the one skilled trade covered in this book that typically doesn't require a high school diploma (or equivalent credential). The training to become a laborer is provided while on the job, with new workers watching and learning from experienced workers. A diploma *is* usually required in order to do certain specialized work on-site, such as helping electricians and plumbers.

Although most construction laborers and helpers begin working for a contractor directly, there are apprenticeship programs for construction laborers that typically last for two years. See the Laborers' International Union of North America (LIUNA) website at www.liuna.org for more information.

The classification of craftsperson covers many specializations within the construction field, including carpenter, welder, roofer, solar cell installer, painter, drywall installer, tile installer, equipment operator, inspector, boilermaker, and many others. Entering one of these professions usually requires a high school diploma or equivalent credential. Many people in these professions start out as laborers and then move up as they learn the ropes from seasoned craftspeople. As is the case for plumbers, electricians, and HVAC technicians, these jobs usually involve on-the-job training, which means completing an apprenticeship program (normally two years) and, in some cases, passing an exam.

Construction managers plan, budget, and supervise construction projects. These jobs pay much higher salaries. Coming up through the ranks into management is certainly possible, but bear in mind that in almost all cases these jobs require a four-year bachelor's degree. When seeking managers to hire, construction companies and contractors usually look for people who have both a degree in a relevant area (such as construction science, building science, or engineering) plus some on-the-job experience in construction.

AUTO SERVICE TECHNICIAN/MECHANIC

Becoming an auto service technician or mechanic requires a high school diploma (or equivalent credential) as well as specialized vocational training after high school. The normal path to this career involves completing a program in automotive service technology, which usually lasts six months to a year, before being hired. The ability to tinker with cars, fiddle with electronics, and handle tools is a plus, but it's not enough to find real work in this field.

Before employment can begin, a technician must become certified by the National Institute for Automotive Service Excellence. This certification requires two years of experience on the job or a combination of one year of in-school training and one year on the job. You can find out more information on training and test prep at www.ase.com. Additionally, the Environmental Protection Agency (EPA) requires that anyone who works with refrigerants, including the air-conditioning systems in cars, become certified in proper methods of handling those substances. Most tech training programs will prepare you for this certification.

This field usually involves a lot of contact with customers, sometimes repeatedly and long term. Coursework in customer relations is usually a good idea, as are personal traits such as patience, courtesy, and the ability to listen and answer detailed questions.

Hands-On Requirements

As mentioned in the previous section, many if not most jobs in the skilled trades involve some kind of apprenticeship program. Apprenticeship is a terrific way to gain experience while getting paid at the same time.

HOW APPRENTICESHIP WORKS

In an apprenticeship program, a beginner is guided and taught necessary skills and practices on the job by an experienced employee, often alongside additional training in a classroom setting or through online or correspondence classwork. Apprenticeships are paid positions, though at a much lower rate than journey and master-level workers. At the end of an apprenticeship program, the status of journeyman worker is awarded, meaning you are able to work without supervision and can apply for work pretty much anywhere in the country.

Each of the skilled trades has its own procedures and traditions, and the ways in which apprenticeship is handled may vary among them. However, in general, apprenticeships usually have the following characteristics:

- The program is sponsored by an employer such as a building contractor, a labor union, a joint organization that includes both labor and a company, or an employer association.
- It is recognized as an apprenticeship program in the industry.

A plumber and his apprentice.

- It is open to qualified applicants. The qualifications may vary, but often the applicant must be eighteen years old or older, hold a driver's license, and have earned a high school diploma or equivalent credential.
- It involves around 2,000 hours of on-the-job training and 144 hours of class instruction per year.
- The worker is hired at the apprentice level and paid throughout the program at about half the pay rate of a fully qualified journeyman.
- Completion of the program confers an industry-recognized credential and includes promotion to journeyman level.

FINDING AN APPRENTICESHIP PROGRAM

There are a few ways to start looking for an apprenticeship program. An easy way to get started is to check with your school or community librarian for resources on local apprenticeships, or to ask around among friends and family.

You can also look online. Here are some good links that can help your search:

- *US Department of Labor Apprenticeship Sponsor Database* (https:// oa.doleta.gov/bat.cfm): This site offers fine tools to narrow down apprenticeship programs by location, industry, and sponsoring organization, providing contact information for apprenticeship sponsors in your area.
- *US Department of Labor Apprenticeships* (www.apprenticeship.gov): This government site offers general information on apprenticeship programs for employers and career seekers. It also has articles assessing the state of apprenticeships by industry. You can enter your zip code and find programs within a certain number of miles from your home.
- *CareerOneStop's Apprenticeship Finder* (www.careeronestop.org/Toolkit/ Training/find-apprenticeships.aspx): Similar to the service on the Department of Labor website, here you enter your zip code and the site returns a list of programs in your area.

WHAT IS A REGISTERED APPRENTICESHIP?

The US Department of Labor sets out national standards for apprenticeships and registers programs that meet those standards. In order to meet the standards, an apprenticeship must pay the apprentice, must conform to certain guidelines issued by the Department of Labor, must foster learning and provide technical instruction on the job, and must assign an employee of the company to direct the apprenticeship. The Department of Labor bestows an industry-recognized credential at the completion of a registered apprenticeship program. Find out more about registered apprenticeships at www.dol.gov/featured/apprenticeship/faqs.

Networking

There's an old saying: "It's not what you know, it's who you know." And actually, in many cases, it's really who *they* know. Networking is a way to cultivate a web of relationships and use those relationships to make new ones. The connections and affiliations between people and groups of people make up what's called a social network. Social networking is powerful and has become very important in the modern workplace.

THE CONCEPT OF SOCIAL NETWORKING

Imagine you have ten contacts in your social network. You could represent yourself as a dot in the middle, and your contacts as ten dots arranged in a circle around you. Then you could draw a line connecting you to each of them, like spokes on a bike wheel. Now imagine that each of your contacts knows ten people. Draw ten dots in a circle around each of the original ten dots and lines connecting those dots to their new dots. And of course, each of those *new* dots would also have ten dots, and so on.

What happened here, and what does it mean? It means your original ten contacts could potentially introduce you to one hundred new contacts. And *those* contacts could then introduce you to one thousand new contacts. As you can see, this simple concept swiftly starts adding up to big numbers. In fact, you would only have to go through three more rounds of drawing dots and you would be looking at more than a million people. And this example is conservative. Ten is a pretty small number to start with. You probably know a lot more than ten people, and each of them surely does, too.

This should give you a sense of the tremendous power of networking and why it's a major force in the business world. You can use networking as part of your work, and you can use it to find work. For example, I found all the tradespeople interviewed for this book (including Andy, the plumber you'll read about later in this chapter) through my own social network—in this case, Facebook (www.facebook.com). I posted a single request asking if anyone knew someone in the specific skilled trades who might be interested in being interviewed for a book, and in less than one hour I had identified and contacted all five of them.

A social network maps the relationships among people and groups.

LinkedIn (www.linkedin.com) is a professional networking website specifically designed as a tool for cultivating business contacts. You can sign up for a free account on the website, and once you're signed up, you can start adding your own connections—the more, the better. You can search the site for positions and job titles, and LinkedIn will show you job openings and potential contacts who are contacts of your own contacts. In this way you can grow your number of professional contacts very quickly.

HOW TO NETWORK

Let's go back to the beginning, to those first ten dots you imagined drawing. Who are they? You are likely a young person without a lot of experience or contacts in the career field you may be interested in. How can you possibly network your way into a job in that field from where you are now?

Well, take a minute to really consider all the people you know. To begin with, you can probably count some or all of the following among your contacts right now:

- Parents
- Extended family members (aunts and uncles, cousins, perhaps grandparents)
- Friends (plus their parents and older siblings)
- Social media friends (Instagram, Snapchat, Twitter, Facebook, and so on)
- Teachers
- School administrators
- Coaches, club leaders, and sponsors (band, student council, yearbook)
- Clergy (pastor, rabbi, imam, priest)
- Employers and former employers
- Coworkers and former coworkers
- Neighbors
- Fellow church or club members (people you know from church or local clubs like 4-H, Lion's Club, Elks and Moose lodges, or Knights of Columbus)

Suddenly, it seems that you actually know quite a few people. Now imagine how many people *they* know.

You probably have an address book of some kind. If not, you can pick one up at a drug store or supermarket. Start writing down your contacts' names, phone numbers, and e-mail addresses. In many cases, you may only have a name. That's okay for now—write those down, too. These single names can serve as placeholders until you get their phone numbers and e-mail addresses.

Once you have a good number of contacts written down, come up with a short statement that says what kind of help you're looking for. For example, something like this:

> Hi, _____. I'm looking for contacts in the _____ field as I consider my career choices. I am wondering if you might know someone I could talk to about this, to expand my network as I look for training and job opportunities? If you know of anyone who might be of help and you feel comfortable passing along their contact info, I would truly appreciate it!

Save your statement in generic form and then paste it into e-mails, instant messages, or text messages and customize it as appropriate each time—*don't* forget to customize it. If you prefer speaking on the phone, prepare a similar brief appeal that you can deliver verbally. Be brief, but don't be shy. Most people are more than willing to help if they can. Try to contact five people per day. That's enough to start making progress on expanding your network, but it's not enough to be overwhelming or burdensome. In no time, your address book will be filling up. For example, by the end of the first week you will have contacted thirty-five people and may have collected that many—or more—new contacts.

Once you've made a new contact, use a similar script or speech with that person, being sure to mention your common acquaintance by name. See if he or she is available to meet to discuss the career, training, and job opportunities you're interested in. If your meeting goes well, don't hesitate to ask if he or she knows of someone else you may want to talk to.

DON'T FORGET YOUR LOCAL ELECTED LEADERS

You may not know your elected leaders personally, but in a way you sort of do. After all, *you're their boss.* At age eighteen you can become a voter, and these people have to pay some attention to voters. If you're even a little bit of an outgoing type, you can use this situation to your advantage.

Even if you live in a small town, there is probably at least a mayor, a few commissioners, and a city council. In a mid-sized city, you've got all those people, plus several city departments and probably a state representative or state senator with an office not too far away. In a bigger city or state capital, you'll have more bureaus and offices and departments than you'll know what to do with—not to mention your US representatives and/or senators, who may also have offices nearby. If you're not sure who they are or how to find them, a good place to start is www.usa.gov/elected-officials.

Can these important people really become part of your professional network? You bet they can. You may be surprised at how easy it is to get an appointment to talk with a local official. All you have to do is find the number, call, and ask. The worst they can say is no, and if they do, remind them that you vote—then try someone else.

If they say yes, be sure to dress nicely and be on time. Bring a notebook and a pen. Introduce yourself and get right to the point. These people are busy. Say you're looking to begin a career in whichever skilled trade interests you and you're wondering if they could connect you with someone who works in that field or is involved in vocational education who could help you.

Don't worry that you're wasting their valuable time. They will have ten meetings after you and will forget you by the end of the day. Also, helping young people is actually one part of the job that many officials find rewarding and satisfying. Be friendly and direct—try not to act shy. An official who agrees to meet with you will likely see you as a very easy problem to solve compared to the rest of what's on his or her plate that day. Don't be surprised if he or she immediately offers to recommend you to two or three people. These may even be important-sounding people, like the city electric commissioner or head of a local factory or sewage or power plant.

With any luck, you will leave your (short) meeting with at least one contact whom you can then follow up with, using your official as an impressive-sounding reference. If you're worried about what makes you special enough to get important leaders to meet with you, don't be. You were likely one of the few to think of doing this, let alone get up the nerve to act on it—well done! (Chapter 4 has more information on interviewing.)

THE PRIDE AND SATISFACTION OF PLUMBING

Andrew Dixon.
Courtesy of Andrew Dixon

Andrew Dixon is a plumber for Halloran and Yauch Irrigation in Chicago, Illinois. He is a twenty-eight-year member of Chicago Journeyman Plumbers Local Union 130 and is licensed and certified to test cross-connection devices. A certified green plumber, Andy has also held welding and medical gas certifications in the past. He holds an associate's degree in metallurgical engineering from a local community college, where he trained and went to school through the union, spending three years in school and five years in apprenticeship.

Why did you choose to become a plumber?

In the past I worked with a company called Great Lakes Plumbing and Heating, on high-rise construction. I worked building dental offices, commercial kitchens, car washes, retail build-outs, and municipal water systems, to name a few. I also volunteered for Habitat for Humanity, installing solar thermal systems. After I went to college, I worked as an auto mechanic. It was suggested to me that I should apply for apprenticeship with the plumbers. I did, and here I am thirty years later.

What is a typical day on the job for you?

It starts early. I'm awake at 4:00 or 4:30 a.m., rain or shine. I either start at the shop or at a job site. If I am going to the shop, I meet with the company owners and receive a briefing. I gather materials, safety gear, machines, and manpower that I will need. I drive a work truck to the job site and begin assessing the situation and working a plan of installation. I contact plumbing inspectors, property owners (if a water shutdown is needed), and utility-finding services. Typical municipal irrigation systems would begin with finding the water main and digging it up, dropping a trench box in the hole to work without the fear of a trench collapse, pumping out groundwater and performing a water main tap. I typically install valves, roll out soft copper, and flare the copper and trench to a spot designated on a set of plans. I'll have the work inspected and backfill with specific materials. I determine finished grade, figure out the size of a concrete pad, and check the plans for dimensions of an enclosure. I then install valves and water meters, backflow prevention devices, and pumps.

What's the best part of your job?

Easy—it is satisfaction. I have been trained with the best and have had great instruction. My standards are extremely high. My work is my signature. I strive to do the best possible job. I change venues often, so I don't get bored being stuck at the same location for too long. I take great pride teaching young apprentices the craft and passing along the tradition of expertise.

What's the worst or most challenging part of your job?

The toll that years of work take on the body. Arthritis, tendonitis, pinched nerves, sunburn, and frostbite. It isn't easy. It is the years of experience that make it look easy.

What's the most surprising thing about your job?

The fact that people think that plumbers just fix toilets and sinks. I try and learn all the time. I am constantly training, because the industry is always changing. I spend a significant amount of my personal time learning and keeping ahead of my work.

What's next? Where do you see yourself going from here?

Retirement. In retirement I will be volunteering to build sustainable housing. I'll be helping the poor to have clean, safe water.

Did your education prepare you for the job?

Yes. I use mathematics and geometry every day. Just being in school taught me how to be specific and how to communicate with people and superiors.

Is the job what you expected?

No. Work can be exciting. I sometimes go months focusing on projects, oftentimes bypassing things that I normally enjoy so that I can spend more time preparing and being 100 percent ready to have all the answers.

Summary

This chapter explored the steps involved in forming a career plan. First, you considered your own personality traits, skills, and interests, and asked yourself several questions to help guide your way toward pursuing a career path that is likely to be successful. Remember: Your happiness is the overall goal.

You read about websites and organizations that can serve as resources as you form your career plan. There is a wealth of helpful information available to you as you begin this journey. You were also encouraged to take advantage of the resources you have through your school, including guidance counselors.

You read about which high school classes are best suited to prepare for a career in the skilled trades, with an emphasis on science and math classes and any vocational courses your school may offer. You then looked at the typical educational requirements for each of the five skilled trades careers covered in this book. Almost all of them require a high school diploma and some additional coursework, which may or may not lead to a degree such as an associate's degree. Many of these careers offer on-the-job training programs called apprenticeships, which provide trainees the necessary experience to work independently, an industry-recognized credential, and greatly enhanced employment prospects.

This chapter covered the concept of networking, including how social and professional networks work and how to harness them to your advantage as you embark on a career path. It also shared some ideas about how to expand your network of contacts.

Next, chapter 3 will walk you step-by-step through fulfilling the educational requirements for many skilled trades.

Pursuing the Education Path

*W*hen it comes time to start looking at vocational schools—also called technical schools or career colleges—many high schoolers tend to freeze up at the enormity of the job ahead of them. This chapter will help break down this process for you so it won't seem so daunting.

Finding the right learning institution is important, and it's a big step on your career path. The last chapter covered the various educational requirements of these five skilled trades careers, which means you should now be ready to find the right institution of learning. This isn't always just a process of finding the very best school that you can afford and can be accepted into, although that might end up being your path. It should also be about finding the right fit so that you can have the best possible experience.

Attending postsecondary schooling isn't just about completing the program requirements or even getting an associate's degree. It's also about learning how to be an adult, managing your life and your responsibilities, being exposed to new experiences, growing as a person, and otherwise becoming someone who contributes to society.

An important component of how successful you will be in your postsecondary education is finding the right school that brings out the best in you and challenges you at different levels. Just as with finding the right profession, your ultimate goal should be to match your personal interests, goals, and personality with the program's own characteristics. For example, a technical institute in a nearby big city will have a different feel than a rural or suburban community college or an online vocational program.

Finding a Vocational School That Fits Your Personality

Before getting into the details of which schools to look at for each of the skilled trades, you may want to take a minute to consider which type of school might be best for you. Granted, you may not have a lot of choice. You could be limited in terms of how close the school must be to where you live, especially if you have a day (or night) job or family responsibilities. In those cases, you'll probably have to choose between what's fairly close by and an online program. And that's fine, as long as the school is up to snuff and delivers what it promises (more on that later).

If you do have at least a few choices, though, thinking about the following things can help you narrow your search. You can do almost all of your research on these characteristics through the schools' websites. If you don't find what you're looking for there, don't hesitate to call the school and ask.

- *Community location:* Would you prefer to be in a rural area, a small town, a suburban area, or a large city? How important is the location of the school in the larger world?
- *Distance from home:* How far away from home—in terms of hours or miles away—are you willing to go?
- *Student body:* How would you like the student body to look? Does the school encourage females and minorities to apply? How many students are part-time versus full-time? What percentage commutes?

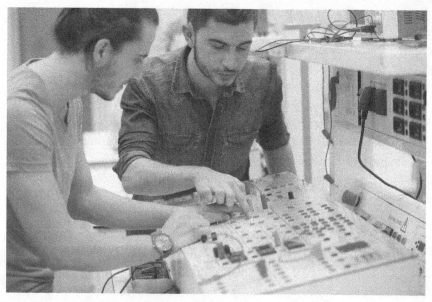

Students working on an electronic circuit board in vocational class.

- *Academic environment:* Consider which subjects and programs are offered and at which degree levels. Does the school have numerous programs in many subjects, or does it focus just on, for example, electrician training? Find out about the school's affiliation with apprenticeship programs.
- *Outcomes:* What percentage of students drop out? What percentage end up gainfully employed in the career for which they trained?
- *Financial aid availability/cost:* Does the school provide ample opportunities for scholarships, grants, work-study programs, and the like? How much does cost play a role in your options? (More about financial aid later in this chapter.)
- *Support services:* How strong are the school's academic and career placement counseling services? Also find out how well stocked with updated equipment their shop and lab areas are.
- *Specialized programs:* Does the school offer programs for veterans or students with disabilities or special needs?

US News & World Report says that the college that fits you best is one that:

- Offers a degree that matches your interests and needs
- Provides a style of instruction that matches the way you like to learn
- Provides a level of academic rigor to match your aptitude and preparation
- Offers a community that feels like home to you
- Values you for what you do well

Take some time to paint a mental picture about the kind of school setting that will best complement your needs. Then read on for specifics about each degree or credential.

"It's instant gratification to be able to stand back at the end of the day or project and see the progress I've made. It's satisfying to provide a service that most individuals are not capable of doing themselves or have no desire to do themselves."
—Tom Moser, painting contractor

WHAT'S THE DIFFERENCE BETWEEN VOCATIONAL SCHOOL AND COLLEGE?

Both vocational school and college provide postsecondary (after high school) education, and both award degrees, but there are some pretty big differences:

- Colleges and universities are designed for four-year bachelor's and graduate degree programs. Vocational schools are geared toward two-year associate's degrees and various certificates for study lasting less than two years.
- In college, students take a wide variety of courses, some of which are outside their area of study. In vocational school, students study one subject with a narrow focus and an emphasis on practical training for a specific job. This is why it only takes two years instead of four.
- A large percentage of college students live on or very near campus. Most vocational students commute to class, and many hold down outside jobs.
- Colleges and universities cost significantly more to attend, often two or three times what vocational schools cost.
- At a vocational college, you won't see huge lecture halls filled with a couple hundred students taking notes on a lecture by a professor who doesn't know their names. Classes at vocational schools are usually small (twenty to thirty students) and often involve hands-on training in shops and labs.

Determining Your Education Plan

The skilled trades discussed in this book, except for construction laborer or helper, have somewhat different requirements for vocational education and training. These requirements may also vary by state or municipality. Check with your school or your state's department of labor website or licensing board. This section dives into these educational programs for each of the skilled trades.

ELECTRICIAN

Most states require electricians to have completed some combination of classroom instruction and work experience in order to become licensed to work on high-voltage electrical systems such as those found in homes and offices. That's one reason why an apprenticeship is an excellent way to become an electrician—it offers exactly that school-work combination. Apprenticeship programs also often require some vocational training in order to apply.

There are generally two levels of education available in vocational school electrical programs:

- *Certificate or diploma:* These are programs of coursework that last a semester or two (six months to a year). They feature a lot of hands-on training and focus on purely technical and theoretical topics directly relating to the job of an electrician.
- *Degree:* These are usually two-year programs that include more general and varied related coursework on top of the focused technical training.

Which route you choose to take is up to you. Your decision may depend on how eager you are to get to work. Completing a certificate or diploma program (in six months to a year) will probably be enough for you to gain acceptance into an apprenticeship program, which then may take three to five more years. However, earning a two-year associate's degree is more impressive to apprenticeship programs and may not only increase your chances of being accepted but also allow you to enter an apprenticeship program at a higher level—meaning your apprenticeship period may be shorter.

Vocational school certificate and diploma programs for electricians vary somewhat in what they teach, but almost all will cover the following topics:

- The National Electrical Code (NEC)
- Building codes
- Wiring
- Inspection and troubleshooting
- Electricity and electronics
- Safety measures and precautions
- Maintenance of electrical components

A two-year associate's degree program will include more general education classes in addition to the job-focused technical courses.

Licensing requirements for electricians vary from state to state, so you'll need to find out what the rules and laws are in your area. Typically, you have to complete an apprenticeship program and pass a state exam in order to become a licensed (journeyman) electrician.

WHAT IS A LOW-VOLTAGE OR VOICE-DATA-VIDEO ELECTRICIAN?

When most people think of an electrician, they tend to think of somebody working on dangerous high-voltage systems, like power lines or the power wiring in residential homes and businesses. However, there is another type of electrical work, called low-voltage or voice-data-video, which utilizes wiring that doesn't carry such a high voltage. Low-voltage electricians are technicians who install and repair systems using this kind of wiring, which include:

- Home entertainment systems
- Closed-circuit video systems
- Security systems
- Data and signal wiring such as cable television, fiber optic, computer networking cables, and telephone wiring

Low-voltage work is included in the NEC and in the normal educational and training phases of becoming an electrician. But because working with these systems isn't as dangerous, in some states the licensing and certification may be different or more relaxed. There are also programs that lead to being credentialed specifically as a low-voltage technician.

You can read more about becoming a low-voltage electrician at www.electricianschooledu.org/low-voltage-electrician.

WHAT IS THE NATIONAL ELECTRICAL CODE?

Problems with electricity are one of the most common causes of fires every year. The NEC is a set of standards and guidelines for electrical systems published periodically by the National Fire Protection Association (NFPA) intended to ensure that electrical systems are as safe as possible. It has been adopted by all fifty states.

The NEC is a book that you study, and the material it covers makes up a significant part of any electrician's licensing exam. It's also the basis by which inspectors certify that electrical systems installed or repaired by electricians are acceptable and safe. The most recent edition of the NEC was published in 2017.

You can read the actual code, if you have a mind to, at www.nfpa.org/codes-and-standards/all-codes-and-standards/list-of-codes-and-standards/detail?code=70.

HVAC TECHNICIAN

HVAC education and training are similar to that for electricians. The typical path is to obtain HVAC training at a vocational school and then enter into an apprenticeship program. The skills needed to work in HVAC are varied and wide-ranging, and include knowing the basics of the sheet metal, electrical, plumbing, welding, and pipefitting trades. That adds up to a lot to study.

There are generally two levels of education available in vocational school HVAC programs:

- *Certificate or diploma:* These are programs of coursework that last a semester or two (six months to a year). They feature a lot of hands-on training and focus on purely technical and theoretical topics directly relating to the job of an HVAC technician.
- *Degree:* These are usually two-year programs that include more general and varied related coursework on top of the focused technical training.

Which route you choose to take is up to you. Your decision may depend on how eager you are to get to work. Completing a certificate or diploma program (in six months to a year) will probably be enough for you to gain acceptance into an apprenticeship program, which then may take three to five more years. However, earning a two-year associate's degree is more impressive to apprenticeship programs and may not only increase your chances of being accepted but also allow you to enter an apprenticeship program at a higher level—meaning your apprenticeship period may be shorter.

Vocational school certificate and diploma programs for HVAC technicians vary somewhat in what they teach, but almost all will cover the following topics:

- HVAC theory
- Electricity and electronics
- Airflow and venting systems
- Building codes and safety practices
- Refrigerants
- Thermostats
- Installation, problem solving, troubleshooting
- Air-conditioning
- Soldering
- Piping

A two-year associate's degree program will include more general education classes in addition to the job-focused technical courses.

Licensing requirements to work as an HVAC technician vary from state to state, so you'll need to find out what the rules and laws are in your area. You may have to pass a state exam. In some states you must also have completed an apprenticeship program before you can become licensed. In all states, anyone working with refrigerants (which means anyone working on air conditioners) must pass the EPA Section 608 written certification exam. You can read more about this exam at www.epa.gov/section608/section-608-technician-certification-test-topics.

PLUMBER

Plumbing education and training are similar to those for electricians and HVAC technicians, with a few differences. The typical path is to enroll in a plumbing program at a vocational school and then enter into an apprenticeship plumber program.

There are generally two levels of education available in vocational school plumbing programs:

- *Certificate or diploma:* These are programs of coursework that last a semester or two (six months to a year). They feature a lot of hands-on training and focus on purely technical and theoretical topics directly relating to the job of a plumber.
- *Degree:* These are usually two-year programs that include more general and varied related coursework on top of the focused technical training.

Which route you choose to take is up to you. Your decision may depend on how eager you are to get to work. Completing a certificate or diploma program (in six months to a year) will probably be enough for you to gain acceptance into an apprenticeship program, which then may take three to five more years. However, earning a two-year associate's degree is more impressive to apprenticeship programs and may not only increase your chances of being accepted but also allow you to enter an apprenticeship program at a higher level—meaning your apprenticeship period may be shorter.

Vocational school certificate and diploma programs for plumbers vary somewhat in what they teach, but almost all will cover the following topics:

- Fundamentals of plumbing
- Piping systems
- Welding and soldering
- Plumbing codes and safety practices
- Chemistry and math
- Installation, problem solving, troubleshooting

A two-year associate's degree program will include more general education classes in addition to the job-focused technical courses.

Licensing requirements to work as a plumber vary from state to state, so you'll need to find out what the rules and laws are in your area. In some states you must obtain a license before even beginning an apprenticeship program. States tend to offer three levels of licensing exams, corresponding to the three levels of plumbing (apprentice, journeyman, and master).

CONSTRUCTION LABORER, CRAFTSMAN, OR MANAGER

The term *construction* can be applied to a lot of different jobs. Likewise, your educational plan will be different according to the general career level you'd like to reach:

- *Laborers or helpers (high school diploma, on-the-job training):* Generally a high school degree is helpful but not required for these jobs, which involve carrying, lifting, hauling, and cleaning up construction sites, and assisting other workers, including craftspeople.
- *Craftspeople (1–2 years vocational, 2–4 years apprenticeship):* These skilled workers include specialists like painters, carpenters, masons, machine operators, drillers, and welders. A high school degree is usually required along with additional postsecondary vocational technical training and/or apprenticeship programs. Craftspeople earn significantly more than laborers.
- *Managers (bachelor's degree and construction experience):* In most cases, a bachelor's degree from a college or university is required in order to become a construction manager. A manager is typically responsible for managing project budgets and using the company's resources to generate profit from these projects. Managers earn significantly more than craftspeople.

A successful career as a craftsperson such as a carpenter or machine operator often involves a similar level of education and training as an electrician, HVAC technician, or plumber. The usual path involves earning a certificate or diploma from a focused program at a vocational school followed by completion of an apprenticeship program lasting a few years. The apprenticeship is largely on-the-job training directed by an experienced craftsperson such as a licensed carpenter or machine operator.

One path that can pay off later in your career if you want to get into management is to earn an associate's degree in a chosen craft specialty, complete an internship, gain experience as a journeyman working on construction sites, and then complete two more years of schooling (perhaps in the evenings) to earn a bachelor's degree. This combination of extensive work experience in a construction specialty plus the required management credential is very attractive to employers.

That said, there are so many different jobs within the field of construction, it's not possible to give the educational requirements for every one. Some employers may value advanced skills more than formal education. For example, welding is an important part of construction, and good welders are highly sought after. There are welding programs that lead to diplomas and certificates, but if you've already learned welding and can prove your skills, it could be that the right employer will take a chance on you and hire you at the entry level. This could be true for any number of construction/craftsperson jobs, not just welding.

The Bureau of Labor Statistics has a lot of information about typical education plans for many different construction jobs at www.bls.gov/ooh/construction-and-extraction/home.htm.

AUTO SERVICE TECHNICIAN/MECHANIC

As with the other trades, when hiring auto service technicians and mechanics, employers want a certificate/diploma or associate's degree. Most also desire/require Automotive Service Excellence (ASE) certification. Automotive technology programs usually last one or two years and cover the following topic areas (and more):

- Shop safety
- Traits of various manufacturers
- Transmissions
- Air-conditioning/heating systems
- Engines
- Exhaust systems
- Electronics and computer components

- Troubleshooting and diagnostics
- Alignment
- Brakes and tires

Auto repair shops and garages are also usually stand-alone businesses where customers visit, so customer service and business topics are also found in these programs. For example, courses covering the following are typically offered:

- Warranties
- Bookkeeping
- Writing orders
- Customer relations
- Estimating costs

Generally, a two-year associate's degree program in automotive technology is advisable, as it can both make you attractive to employers and prepare you for ASE certification, including the hands-on-training experience requirement.

Automotive technology programs sometimes partner with local businesses to create a kind of apprenticeship program, which allows students to get more hands-on training as part of their coursework.

WHAT IS ASE CERTIFICATION?

Automotive professionals in the United States are certified by the National Institute for Automotive Service Excellence, an independent nonprofit organization. ASE certification promotes high standards and quality service among auto service techs and mechanics, both protecting consumers and ensuring employers that their hires indeed have the right skill set. ASE certification has two requirements:

- Two years of on-the-job training or one year of on-the-job-training and a two-year associate's degree in automotive repair
- Passing the ASE certification test

The test is hard, and you must retake it every five years in order to remain certified because auto technology changes so quickly.

You can find out more about ASE certification (and even register for the test) at www.ase.com.

Schools and Apprenticeships

Once you've narrowed down your choices to decide on one of the skilled trade careers and have a sense of what kind of schooling and training is required in order to get your first job in the field, it's time to start considering your real-world options. In practical terms, this means finding a vocational school and, in many cases, an apprenticeship.

For example, to become an electrician, HVAC technician, or plumber, you might look for a vocational program you can complete and an internship program you can get into. To become an automotive service technician and mechanic, you pretty much just need to find a vocational program in automotive technology. For construction jobs, a laborer or helper position will likely not require any further education; a craftsperson position will require finding a vocational program and (perhaps) an internship; and a management job will require that you eventually earn a four-year bachelor's degree. Table 3.1 sums up these requirements.

The rest of this section will cover finding the best schools and internships to fit your chosen career path.

Table 3.1. Typical School and Apprenticeship Requirements by Trade

Job Title	Education	Internship	Certification/License
Electrician	1–2-year vocational	3–5 years	NEC (plus local, if required)
HVAC Technician	1–2-year vocational	3–5 years	EPA 608 (plus local, if required)
Plumber	1–2-year vocational	3–5 years	May vary by state
Auto Service Technician	1–2-year vocational	No	ASE
Construction Laborer	High school	No	None
Construction Crafts-person	1–2-year vocational	2–4 years	May vary by state
Construction Manager	4-year bachelor's degree	No	None

FINDING GOOD VOCATIONAL SCHOOLS

As of 2016, there were roughly twenty-four hundred two-year colleges, vocational schools, and other technical schools in the United States.[1] That's a lot to choose from. How do you know which ones are good? A school's accreditation is intended to help distinguish schools that meet high educational standards from those that don't. Generally, accreditation means some authority has evaluated the school and publicly ensures that the school's educational standards are high. Unfortunately, there are a few different types of accreditation, and they mean slightly different things.

Most state colleges and universities are regionally accredited. There are six such regions in the United States, and a different regional educational association handles accrediting for the schools in each region. These regional accreditations are recognized by the US Department of Education and the Council for Higher Education Accreditation. Credits from a regionally accredited school are also transferable to a four-year college or university. This means if you earn an associate's degree from a regionally accredited school and later want to complete your bachelor's degree, your two years of credits will transfer successfully.

There are also nationally accredited schools—which sounds even better, but may not be. A few different organizations issue national accreditations to these schools, which are typically more specialized and narrowly focused, such as many programs teaching the trade careers. Nationally accredited schools will accept credit transfers from regionally accredited schools, but not the other way around. Keep that in mind when choosing a school if you think you may want to finish a four-year degree someday.

You can check to see whether a school is accredited by entering its name into the search box at the following Department of Education website: https://ope.ed.gov/dapip/#/home. The Council for Higher Education Accreditation also has a searchable database of accredited schools at www.chea.org. The FTC has a helpful guide to choosing a reputable, high-quality vocational school at www.consumer.ftc.gov/articles/0241-choosing-vocational-school.

To get a list of accredited schools near you, you can check the comprehensive database maintained by the Council for Higher Education Accreditation. Follow these steps:

1. Go to www.chea.org/search-institutions.
2. Make sure the Country box says United States.
3. In the State box, choose your state.
4. In the City box, type the name of your city or the nearest large city. (This is optional, and it may limit the results you get. If you leave it blank, you'll get all the accredited schools in your state.)
5. Look through the list and click the Visit Website links for the schools that interest you.

There are also lots of databases available on the internet that offer lists of more specific career programs (like plumber or electrician). Here are two that are fairly reliable:

- Trade Schools Guide (www.trade-schools.net)
- Accredited Schools Online (www.accreditedschoolsonline.org/vocational-trade-school)

Of course, you can also enter "*job* trade schools *city or state name*" into your favorite search engine (replacing *job* with whatever your chosen trade is, and adding your city or state name). You'll get a lot of hits—use your usual healthy dose of caution and skepticism when clicking the offered links.

Another way to find good schools is to look at school rankings. The gold standard for postsecondary school rankings is the widely publicized annual list put out by the magazine *US News & World Report*. Unfortunately, the magazine doesn't rank vocational or technical training schools or junior colleges offering two-year associate's degrees.

Forbes magazine does rank these schools, but it includes schools offering programs of all types, such as healthcare and agriculture, not just the skilled trades. (If you're curious about what it says about the best overall two-year trade schools in the country in 2018, you can read *Forbes*'s rankings at www.forbes.com/sites/cartercoudriet/2018/08/15/the-top-25-two-year-trade-schools-colleges-that-can-solve-the-skills-gap/#3590e1b33478.)

When looking at vocational schools—which may include trade schools, technical schools, junior and community colleges, and even branches of four-year colleges and universities—at a minimum you are looking for the following qualities:

- The school should be accredited (regionally or nationally) and licensed.
- The graduation rate (the percentage of students who finish with a degree) should be high.
- The employment or rate of job placement for graduates should be high.
- The tuition should be reasonable, and/or financial aid of some kind should be available.

YOUR PERSONAL STATEMENT

When you apply to a vocational school, in addition to asking for your contact information, educational history, work history, and all sorts of other things, the application may request a personal statement. If so, really take your time with it and give it a lot of thought. Write something that conveys your understanding of the career you're interested in, as well as your desire to practice in this field. This is a chance to stand out among your peers who are also applying.

Why are you uniquely qualified? Why are you a good fit for this program? Your required statement may be short or fairly long (be sure to follow the directions), but whatever the requirements, don't be afraid to make it personal. After all, it's called a *personal* statement. Show it to friends and family, put it away for a few days and then come back to it, revise it, and proofread it. Have other people proofread it. In fact, you may want to ask a professional (such as your school writing center or your local library services) to proofread it. Make sure the admissions professionals who read your statement, along with those of so many other applicants, come away with a snapshot of who you really are and what you are passionate about.

Look online for some examples of good personal statements, which will give you a feel for what works. Be sure to check your specific school for length guidelines, format requirements, and any other guidelines you are expected to follow.

The next section breaks down school rankings by each of the skilled trades. As with accreditation, no one single entity or authority reliably provides such rankings. The rankings here are drawn from various different sources and should be taken with a grain of salt. Still, they should provide at least some examples of pretty good schools.

> If none of the schools listed in this section happens to be located near you, one thing you can do is carefully compare programs that *are* near you with a few of these highly ranked programs. It will take some work on your part, but you can compare things like tuition, graduation rates, employment rates for graduates, length of programs, credential awarded, and so on. You can also check out online programs, covered later in this chapter.

Best Electrician Schools

The following list of the top ten vocational programs for electricians in 2018–2019 comes from Accredited Schools Online,[2] an organization that helps students find accredited schools and make informed decisions.

1. Washburn Institute of Technology, Kansas (www.washburntech.edu)
2. Pamlico Community College, North Carolina (www.pamlicocc.edu)
3. Salina Area Technical College, Kansas (www.salinatech.edu)
4. Central Louisiana Technical Community College (www.cltcc.edu)
5. Alierus Career College, Florida (www.altierus.edu)
6. Mitchell Technical Institute, South Dakota (www.mitchelltech.edu)
7. Cabell County Career Technology Center, West Virginia (http://ctc .cabellschools.com)
8. Weber State University, Utah (www.weber.edu)
9. Siena Heights University, Michigan (www.sienaheights.edu)
10. Northern Michigan University (www.nmu.edu)

Best HVAC Schools

The following list of the top ten vocational programs for HVAC technicians in 2017 comes from College Choice,[3] an education data website.

1. Georgia Piedmont Technical College (www.gptc.edu)
2. Ferris State University, Michigan (www.ferris.edu)
3. Austin Community College, Texas (www.austincc.edu)
4. Northwest Louisiana Technical College (www.nwitc.edu)
5. William Moore College of Technology, Tennessee (www.williamr moore.org)
6. Indian River State College, Florida (www.irsc.edu)
7. Palm Beach State College, Lake Worth, Florida (www.palmbeachstate .edu)
8. Florida State College (www.fscj.edu)
9. Moraine Valley Community College, Illinois (www.morainevalley.edu)
10. Lewis-Clark State College, Idaho (www.lcsc.edu)

Best Plumbing Schools

The following list of the top ten vocational programs for plumbers in 2017–2018 comes from Schools.com,[4] a widely known source of education information.

1. Northern Maine Community College (www.nmcc.edu)
2. Arizona Western College (www.azwestern.edu)
3. Los Angeles Trade Technical College, California (www.lattc.edu)
4. Lee College, Texas (www.lee.edu)
5. Elizabethtown Community and Technical College, Kentucky (www .elizabethtown.kctcs.edu)
6. Thaddeus Stevens College of Technology, Pennsylvania (www.stevens college.edu)
7. St. Cloud Technical and Community College, Minnesota (www.sctcc .edu)
8. Northeast Iowa Community College (www.nicc.edu)
9. SUNY College of Technology at Delhi (www.delhi.edu)
10. Montana State University–Northern (www.msun.edu)

Best Construction Schools

Because construction encompasses many different areas of concentration, it's hard to put together a list of the top schools. The following is a sample of programs offering diplomas, certificates, and associate's degrees in some of the construction trades.

- Alfred State SUNY College of Technology (www.alfredstate.edu)
- Arizona Western College (www.azwestern.edu)
- Central Wyoming College (www.cwc.edu)
- Fort Scott Community College, Kansas (www.fortscott.edu)
- Florida State College (www.fscj.edu)
- Northern Virginia Community College (www.nvcc.edu)
- Portland Community College, Oregon (www.pcc.edu)
- Ivy Tech Community College, Indiana (www.ivytech.edu)
- Fox Valley Technical College, Wisconsin (www.fvtc.edu)
- State Fair Community College, Missouri (www.sfccmo.edu)

Best Automotive Technology Schools

The following list of the top ten automotive technology schools is from the education website TheBestSchools.org.[5]

1. University of Northwest Ohio (www.unoh.edu)
2. Montana State University–Northern (www.msun.edu)
3. Ferris State University, Michigan (www.ferris.edu)
4. Weber State University, Utah (www.weber.edu)
5. Southern Adventist University, Tennessee (www.southern.edu)
6. Utah Valley University (www.uvu.edu)
7. Brigham Young University–Idaho (www.byui.edu)
8. Walla Walla University, Washington (www.wallawalla.edu)
9. Idaho State University (www.isu.edu)
10. Northern Michigan University (www.nmu.edu)

Best Online Vocational Schools

Like everything else, vocational schools have gone online. This is a good option if you want to prepare for a trade career but you have a very busy life, such as working a job and taking care of family, or you live too far from any trade school that could provide the training you need. Online programs also give you more control over your time and allow you to work at a pace that fits your lifestyle. The quality of online education has risen dramatically in recent years. There are lots of good online programs to choose from.

Always check the website of any school you're interested in for information on its online programs. The school may offer a sample that allows you to test drive the virtual classroom instruction and video streaming. Read carefully how the program is set up and how assignments are handled. Is it all electronic, or will you be mailing things back and forth? Will you be meeting with other nearby students?

Make sure you have a decent computer. Most schools list the minimum computing requirements in their program descriptions. You probably won't have to buy much software, because schools use free and open source software whenever possible, but be sure to check. Look into the support the school offers, too. Is someone on staff available to answer questions and troubleshoot problems 24/7? Is help available via online chat or phone (or both)?

Finally, see if you can talk to current or former students who completed the program. Ask them how they liked it, whether they encountered any problems, and whether they would recommend it.

> Be wary of private for-profit schools. Some of these schools have been found to overcharge students and misrepresent graduation and job placement rates. They also tend to cost more in the long run and leave students holding more debt. You can read more details on what to watch out for when it comes to for-profit schools at www.onlinecolleges.net/for-students/for-profit-colleges-student-guide.

The following list of accredited not-for-profit schools offering online vocational programs was compiled in 2018 by Accredited Schools Online,[6] an organization that helps students find accredited schools and make informed decisions.

1. Pamlico Community College, North Carolina (www.pamlicocc.edu)
2. Utica College, New York (www.utica.edu)
3. Liberty University, Virginia (www.liberty.edu)
4. University of Florida (www.ufl.edu)
5. Temple University, Pennsylvania (www.temple.edu)
6. Siena Heights University, Michigan (www.sienaheights.edu)
7. Louisiana State University (www.lsu.edu)

8. St. Catherine University, Minnesota (http://stkate.edu)
9. Alexandria Technical & Community College, Minnesota (http://alex tech.edu)
10. Western Carolina University, North Carolina (www.wcu.edu)

Even if these schools don't offer the exact program you want, you can use them to see what good online schools are doing right. You can look at the different online programs offered and see what appeals to you—then look for those things in schools that have online programs in your chosen field.

FINDING GOOD APPRENTICESHIPS

As you know by now, many skilled trades use an apprenticeship system to supplement classroom instruction with hands-on training devoted to directly learning different aspects of the job. Most apprenticeships require a high school diploma and a year or two of vocational training in order to apply. Apprenticeships usually last two to five years and pay apprentices a wage ($15 an hour on average)[7] while they learn the ropes. The apprentice is guided and supervised during this time by a journeyman—someone who has five or more years of experience, can work independently at the trade, and works for the employer paying the wages.

Apprenticeships are typically sponsored by labor unions, industry associations, employers, and other organizations. Some apprenticeships are also partnerships with vocational schools, community colleges, and universities. The details of how each program works vary among the different careers within the skilled trades. According to the Department of Labor, more than one thousand occupations currently involve apprenticeships.[8] As of 2017, there were more than half a million apprentices currently learning and earning their way toward their chosen careers.[9]

There are several ways to find apprenticeships:

- Check the big online job-hunting sites like Indeed.com (www.indeed .com) and Monster.com (www.monster.com). For example, at Indeed .com you type in your city or zip code in the Where box. In the What search box begin typing something like "electric"—and the choice "electrician's apprentice" will appear as a link. Clicking that link will bring up local electrician apprenticeship programs.
- Look in your local employment classifieds and on Craigslist (www .craigslist.org), where many apprenticeship programs advertise.

- Check with your state's apprenticeship authority (usually a part of your state's department of labor). To find your state's officials who handle registered apprenticeship programs, go to www.careeronestop.org and enter the occupation you're seeking, along with your state. Click Search, and contact information for your state's labor officials who work with apprenticeships will appear.
- You can look for apprenticeships in your chosen trade by going to the Apprenticeship Finder at the Department of Labor website (www .apprenticeship.gov/apprenticeship-finder) and entering your chosen position (for example, "automotive technician") and your zip code. You can read more about the Department of Labor's registered apprenticeship program in chapter 2.
- For those on the electrician path, the International Brotherhood of Electrical Workers (IBEW, www.ibew.org) works in partnership with the National Electrical Contractors Association (NECA, www.neca .org). You may be able to find electrical apprenticeships through the Electrical Training Alliance website at www.electricaltrainingalliance .org, or try the Independent Electrical Contractors (IEC) website at www.myelectriccareer.com.

Successful completion of an apprenticeship program typically confers an industry-recognized credential signifying your entry into journeyman status and making you more marketable. If you stay on with the employer who provided your apprenticeship, you should begin earning a higher salary. And who knows—you may begin training new apprentices yourself!

You can begin looking for apprenticeships at any point in your career journey—you don't have to wait until you finish your diploma, certificate, or degree to begin searching. In fact, the earlier you start reaching out to apprenticeship programs, the better. If you have already talked to someone about an apprenticeship early on, they may remember you favorably when it comes time to formally apply. In some cases, you may find an apprenticeship that will consider taking you on before you finish your vocational program. If that happens, you'll have to weigh the benefits of starting your on-the-job training early versus the benefits of completing your degree.

CHECK WITH YOUR LOCAL UNIONS

Unions are among the most enthusiastic backers of apprenticeships and sponsor many of them. Here are some of the major unions that represent the skilled trades covered in this book. You can use their websites to find your local or lodge, the branch that operates in your area, and contact them about internships:

- International Brotherhood of Electrical Workers (www.ibew.org), represents electricians
- United Association (UA, www.ua.org), represents plumbers and HVAC technicians
- North America's Building Trades Unions (NABTU, www.nabtu.org), represents construction trades
- Laborers' International Union of North America (www.liuna.org), represents construction trades
- International Association of Machinists and Aerospace Workers (IAM, www.unionmechanic.org), represents auto mechanics

There are also lots of smaller regional and local unions scattered about the country. The fastest way to find them is to enter your city or state name, job title (plumber, construction, and so on), and the words "local union" into your favorite search engine.

THE JOY OF PAINTING

Tom Moser. *Courtesy of Tom Moser*

Tom Moser is the owner/operator of Moser's Painting in Weaverville, North Carolina, which he started in 2007. Prior to that he worked for a number of residential painting contractors.

Why did you choose to become a painter?

It started out as seasonal/summer employment while in college. I found I enjoyed spending the summers outside and working with my hands while learning a new skill.

What is a typical day on the job for you?

As a working owner, there is no "typical" day. Every day is something a little different. Some days will be spent doing estimates, meeting with potential customers, getting an understanding of the scope of work to be completed. I'll take measurements to figure out a dollar amount to charge for labor and get an idea of the quantity and total materials needed to complete the job. I then type an estimate and present it to the potential customer. Once they agree to hire me for their services, I move to the scheduling phase, which can be tricky because there are so many variables that can't be controlled—weather being the main one. Sometimes projects take longer than expected, and that also affects your schedule. Once the project starts, I'll have plenty of prep work such as pressure washing/cleaning the areas to be painted or stained, scraping loose and peeling paint, filling nail holes with putty, caulking gaps and cracks, and repairing any rotten areas, or possibly removing wallpaper on some interior jobs. Once everything is prepped, the fun part starts: actually applying paint or stain! There are many methods of doing this: brush, roller, sprayer, rag, stain pad, and so on. Depending on the scope of the work to be completed, it usually takes more than one coat.

What's the best part of your job?

Meeting new people and making their homes/business look better than when I arrived. It's instant gratification to be able to stand back at the end of the day or project and see the progress I've made. It's satisfying to provide a service that most individuals are not capable of doing themselves or have no desire to do themselves.

What's the worst or most challenging part of your job?

Scheduling can be very frustrating. So can running into unforeseen things like wallpaper that doesn't want to come off easily. Sometimes it's hard trying to understand what a customer wants, when in fact they may not know exactly what needs to be done. As a business owner I have a hard time saying no, so when a customer wants to add on something to a project and I agree to do it, it can drastically affect my schedule.

What's the most surprising thing about your job?

The pride and gratification I feel when I have completed a project. The customer is happy. After spending a great deal of time in their home, some people "adopt" you as family, and it's almost sad that it has to come to an end. I love the long-term working friendships I make with the homeowners as well as with my employees.

What's next? Where do you see yourself going from here?

I'm already taking that next step. I scaled back my painting company, though I still take on a handful of jobs and use it as side work. I got a CDL (commercial driver's license) and now drive tractor trailers, delivering finished products from New Belgium Brewing to our distribution center. If I weren't doing that, I would incorporate adding handyman services to my business, because many customers ask about getting other tradesman work done, and it would be a great upsale.

Did your education prepare you for the job?

My bachelor's degree in psychology helped me to understand people, which helps when meeting new customers, working with homeowners, and managing employees.

Is the job what you expected?

It's completely what I expected. Sometimes the business side of it can be a little overwhelming and costly (paying for insurance, workers comp premiums, and taxes), but those are all expenses you should be prepared for when owning and operating any business like this.

What's It Going to Cost You?

So, the bottom line: what will your education end up costing you? Of course, this depends on many factors, including the type and length of degree you pursue; whether the school is a private for-profit, private not-for-profit, or public institution; how much in scholarships or financial aid you're able to obtain; your family or personal income; and many other factors. The College Entrance Examination Board tracks and summarizes financial data from colleges and universities all over the United States. (You can find more information at www.collegeboard.org.)

Public two-year colleges usually offer the most education value for your dollar. In 2018, according to the College Board, the average tuition at public two-year colleges in the United States was $3,660.[10] But not all public colleges will offer the program you're looking for. For vocational schools, average tuition depends greatly on where you live. In New Jersey, for example the average vocational school tuition is $9,167, while in New Mexico it's $3,125.[11]

Costs go up every year. Generally speaking, there is about a 3 percent annual increase in tuition. In other words, if you are expecting to attend college two years after this data was collected, you need to add approximately 6 percent to these numbers. The good news is that financial aid and scholarships can help offset tuition costs.

This chapter discusses finding the most affordable path to get the degree you want. Later in this chapter, you'll also learn how to prime the pump and get as much money for school as you can.

FINANCIAL AID

Finding the money to attend trade school—whether a six-month diploma program, a full two-year associate's degree, or a work-at-your-pace online program—may seem overwhelming at first. But you can do it if you have a plan before you actually start applying to college. If you get into your top-choice program, don't let a higher price turn you away. Financial aid can come from many different sources.

Paying for school can take a creative mix of grants, scholarships, and loans.

The good news is that many schools offer incentive or tuition discount aid to encourage students to attend. The market is often competitive in favor of the student, and schools are responding by offering more generous aid packages to a wider range of students than they used to. Here are some basic tips and pointers about the financial aid process:

- Apply for financial aid during your senior year of high school. You must fill out the Free Application for Federal Student Aid (FAFSA) form, which can be filed starting October 1 of your senior year until June of the year you graduate. Because the amount of available aid is limited, it's best to apply as soon as you possibly can. Go to https://studentaid .ed.gov/sa/fafsa to get started and to find out lots more about the process, including the all-important deadlines for your state.

- Check with each school's financial aid office and be sure to compare and contrast the deals you get from different schools. There is room to negotiate. The first offer of aid may not be the best you'll get.

- Wait until you receive all offers from your top schools and then use this information to negotiate with your top choice to see if they will match or beat the best aid package you received.

- To be eligible to keep and maintain your financial aid package, you must meet certain grade/GPA requirements. Be sure you are very clear about these academic expectations and keep up with them.

- You must reapply for federal aid every year.

Watch out for scholarship scams. You should never be asked to pay to submit the FAFSA form (*free* is in its name) or be required to pay a lot to find appropriate aid and scholarships. These are free services. If an organization promises you you'll get aid or that you have to "act now or miss out," these are warning signs of a less-than-reputable organization.

You should also be careful with your personal information to avoid identity theft as well. Simple things like closing and exiting your browser after visiting sites where you entered personal information goes a long way. Don't share your student aid ID number with anyone, either.

It's important to understand the different forms of financial aid that are available to you. That way, you'll know how to apply for different kinds and get the best financial aid package that fits your needs and strengths.

The two main categories that financial aid falls under are gift aid (such as grants and scholarships), which doesn't have to be repaid, and self-help aid, which includes loans that must be repaid and work-study funds that are earned. The next sections cover the various types of financial aid that fit into these areas.

Grants

Grants typically are awarded to students who have financial needs, but can also be awarded based on other factors, including academics, demographics, veteran support, and special talents. They do not have to be paid back. Grants can come from federal agencies, state agencies, specific universities, and private organizations. Most federal and state grants are based on financial need.

Examples of grants are the Pell Grant, SMART Grant, and the Federal Supplemental Educational Opportunity Grant (FSEOG). Visit the US Department of Education's Federal Student Aid site at https://studentaid.ed.gov/types/grants-scholarships for lots of current information about grants.

Scholarships

Scholarships are merit-based aid that does not have to be paid back. They are typically awarded based on academic excellence. Scholarships can also be athletic-based, minority-based, aid for women, and so forth. These are typically not awarded by federal or state governments, but instead come from the specific school you applied to as well as from private and nonprofit organizations.

Be sure to reach out directly to the financial aid officers of the schools you're interested in. These people are great contacts who can lead you to many more sources of scholarships and financial aid. Visit GoCollege's Financial Aid Finder at www.gocollege.com/financial-aid/scholarships/types for lots more information about how scholarships in general work.

Loans

Many types of loans are available for students to pay for their postsecondary education. Just remember that loans must be paid back, with interest. (This is the extra cost of borrowing the money and is usually a percentage of the amount you borrow.) Be sure you understand the interest rate you will be charged.

Here are some points you need to be clear about before you sign on the dotted line for a loan:

- Is the interest rate fixed or will it change over time?
- Are payments on the loan and interest deferred until you graduate (meaning you don't have to begin paying it off until after you graduate)?
- Is the loan subsidized (meaning the federal government pays the interest until you graduate)?

There are many types of loans offered to students, including need-based loans, non-need-based loans, state loans, and private loans. Two very reputable federal loans are the Perkins Loan and the Direct Stafford Loan.

For more information about student loans, visit https://bigfuture.collegeboard.org/pay-for-college/loans/types-of-college-loans.

Federal Work-Study

The US federal work-study program provides part-time jobs for students with financial need so they can earn money to pay for educational expenses. The focus of such work is on community service work and work related to a student's course of study. Not all schools participate in this program, so be sure to check with the financial aid office at any schools you are considering if this is something you are counting on. The sooner you apply, the more likely you will get the job you desire and be able to benefit from the program, as funds are limited. See https://studentaid.ed.gov/sa/types/work-study for more information about this opportunity.

Making High School Count

If you're still in high school, there are many things you can do now to help the postsecondary educational process go more smoothly. Consider these tips for your remaining years:

- Work on listening well and speaking and communicating clearly. Work on writing clearly and effectively.
- Learn how to learn. This means keeping an open mind, asking questions, asking for help when you need it, taking good notes, and doing your homework.
- Plan a daily homework schedule and keep up with it. Have a consistent, quiet place to study.
- Talk about your career interests with friends, family, and counselors. They may have connections to people in your community who you can shadow or who will mentor you.
- Try new interests and activities, especially during your first two years of high school.
- Be involved in extracurricular activities that truly interest you and that say something about who you are and who you want to be.

When it comes to school, it's a good idea to try working smarter rather than harder. If you're involved in things you enjoy, your educational load won't seem like such a burden. Be sure to take time for self-care, such as sleep, unscheduled down time, meditation, and activities that you find fun and energizing.

Summary

This chapter looked at all the aspects of postsecondary schooling you'll want to consider as you move forward in pursing a career in the skilled trades. Remember that finding the right fit is especially important. The better you feel about a program, the better the chances that you'll stay in school and finish your diploma, certificate, or degree. The five careers covered in this book have varying educational and on-the-job training requirements, which means that finding the right school can be very different depending on your career aspirations.

In this chapter, you learned about some of the impressive schools out there for each of the skilled trades and got some tips on finding a good deal on your education. You were cautioned about what to watch out for, because not all schools are equally forthright and honest about all aspects of the education they're providing. You read about how apprenticeships work, got to know their advantages, and discovered how to find them. You also learned a little about scholarships and financial aid.

Use this chapter as a jumping-off point to dig deeper into your particular area of interest, but don't forget these important points:

- Make sure that the institution you plan to attend has an accredited program in your field of study.
- If you can, get out there and visit some schools in person to get a feel for what they're like. Come prepared to ask questions that aren't addressed on the school website.
- Your personal statement is a very important piece of your application that can set you apart from other applicants. Take the time to make it unique and compelling.
- Don't necessarily assume you can't afford a school based on the sticker price. Many schools offer great scholarships and aid to qualified students. Beyond being a bit of a hassle, it definitely doesn't hurt to apply. This advice especially applies to minorities, veterans, and students with disabilities.
- Spend as much time looking for apprenticeships as you do vocational programs. In most cases, for these careers, it's really the apprenticeship you're after. The schooling is important, but an apprenticeship is your foot in the door to getting paid for doing what you're learning. Look online and in your local media, and don't neglect unions. Union members are often passionate and very involved in the trades and may know of little-publicized avenues into your chosen career.
- Don't lose sight of the fact that it's important to pursue a career that you enjoy, are good at, and are passionate about. You'll be a happier person if you do so.

At this point, you probably have a fairly good idea of your career goals and aspirations. At the very least, you should have a plan for finding out more information. Chapter 4 goes into detail about the next steps: writing a résumé and cover letter, interviewing well, doing follow-up communications, and more. These are key skills in the adult world of work and society. In fact, the sooner you can hone these communication skills, the better off you'll be in the professional world.

4

Writing Your Résumé and Interviewing

*G*etting the required education, training, and apprenticeship experience is important to achieving your career goals in the skilled trades, as you've learned. But it can all be wasted effort if you can't then effectively sell yourself in the job market. Unfortunately, unless you're very lucky, no one is going to come knocking on your door looking for someone like you to hire. That means you need to not just *be* qualified, ready, and capable of taking on a career—you also need to be able to communicate that to school admissions offices, apprenticeship directors, and potential employers. This is true for both your written and verbal communications.

Most apprenticeship and vocational school application processes don't require you to submit a résumé, and most applications for such programs are now online—although some do still require you to fill out actual paperwork, so don't be shocked if you're asked to do that. This chapter therefore assumes you've either already completed, or nearly completed, the education or apprenticeship required by employers. In other words, you're ready to look for a new job, and that means you're trying to get an interview.

You need to know how to build a great résumé and cover letter, interview well with prospective employers, and converse effectively and professionally at all times. The advice in this chapter can definitely help you snag interviews and impress the right people, but the principles discussed here aren't only helpful during your job searches at the beginning of your career. They'll remain important throughout your working life, on and off the job. Learn them now, cultivate them as automatic habits, and they will serve you for as long as you're in the working world.

Writing Your Résumé

Think of your résumé as a one-page ad about yourself. It should summarize—as clearly, effectively, and briefly as possible—your goals, skills, education, and experience. Great résumés also do something else: They give whoever reads them a sense of who the person is and what he or she is like. That's not easy to pull off, but making it happen should be something you shoot for.

PARTS OF A RÉSUMÉ

There are no hard-and-fast rules about exactly what a résumé should contain or how it should look, but a few elements and a certain general look are expected. The basic elements everyone will expect to see on your résumé are as follows, ordered as they normally appear, from top to bottom:

- *Your contact information:* Your name, city and state (or full address), phone number, e-mail address, and social media/personal blog/website. (That last one is optional, and be sure to clean it all up first—more on this potentially disastrous issue later in the chapter.)
- *Your career objective:* This is a short summary or description (one to three sentences) of what you're looking for. As briefly as possible, sum up what you're after and highlight the skills you have for the job.
- *Your skills and qualifications:* Here you should list everything you know how to do that is pertinent to the job, with the most relevant skills first. This is also where you can list certifications or licenses. It's up to you how far you should go in stretching things. For example, if you helped someone tack shingles onto a roof two summers ago, should you put roofing as a skill? A good rule of thumb is to ask yourself, "Would I be comfortable backing this up if they ask about it?" If the answer is yes, go for it.
- *Your experience:* Here you should include the jobs you have held, in reverse chronological order. The first one on your list may well be your current or recent apprenticeship. Don't worry if some of the jobs you've had don't seem particularly relevant to the one you're applying for; include them anyway and do your best to make them seem relevant. You're young, and it's understood that you haven't had a lot of time to

gain direct experience in the field you're entering. Of course, you should emphasize any jobs that *are* especially relevant. Here's where you can also include part-time jobs and volunteer experience.

* *Your education:* Here you should list your vocational schooling history, including any diplomas, certificates, or degrees you've earned.

Sofia Lynch
99 Saturn Avenue
Turtle Creek, Kentucky 42048
555-321-4321 (cell)
sofialynch@email.com

Career objective

Seeking a journey-level electrician position that will leverage my electrical experience and knowledge, critical-thinking skills, facility with tools, and ability to learn quickly.

Skills

* Blueprint/schematics interpretation   * Wiring   * Electrical circuit design
* Conducting electrical inspections   * Safety adherence   * Team collaboration
* Thorough NEC knowledge   * Quality control   * Troubleshooting
* Kentucky licensed electrician

Experience

Apprentice Electrician / Franklin Electric — Turtle Creek, KY (2015–present)
* Repair and install residential and commercial electrical systems
* Implement code requirements and ensure safety compliance
* Conduct diagnostics and troubleshoot faults
* Work on various types of switches and circuits
* Inspect and repair equipment and components
* Estimate repair costs and operate handheld company order-placing technology
* Assist in billing and budgeting

Inventory Specialist / Gadgets & Such — Turtle Creek, KY (2013–2015)
* Organized and received deliveries on loading dock
* Assessed, tracked, revised, and helped manage inventory
* Stocked shelves, helped customers locate
* Assembled tools, machinery, and components for floor display
* Trained new employees on store computer system

Cashier/Server / Pizzapalooza — Lumberton, KY (2011–2013)
* Took orders and worked the till to complete transactions
* Delivered quality product in fast-paced atmosphere
* Handled customer complaints
* Developed strong teamwork skills

Education

* Certificate in Electrical Technology / Ezra Technical College — Ezra, IN (2015)
* High school diploma / Turtle Creek High School — Turtle Creek, KY (2012)

Example résumé for an electrician.

RÉSUMÉ FORMAT, STYLE, AND TONE

It's been said that when employers review a résumé, they're not looking for a reason to hire the person, they're looking for a reason to *reject* them. That sounds mean, but can you figure out why they might do that? It's because even small companies typically receive tons of résumés every week, regardless of whether they currently have jobs advertised. When companies do advertise an open position, they may receive hundreds of résumés in response. Whoever is given the responsibility for reading them simply doesn't have the time to pore over each one in depth.

According to research by the job search site the Ladders (www.theladders .com), a recruiter spends an average of just six seconds reading each résumé.[1] In other words, it takes a job recruiter an average of just six seconds to find an excuse to toss a résumé into the recycling bin. That means your job when writing your résumé is to *not provide any excuse for rejecting it*. Those reasons might be large or small. If your résumé has missing or wrong contact info, typos or spelling errors, confusing dates, or mistaken, missing, or unclear information anywhere, few recruiters will spend any energy or time deciphering it. They'll move on to other résumés.

If you have the computer and writing skills to create your own résumé from scratch using a word-processing program like Microsoft Word, go for it. There are also lots of free résumé-building websites—such as VisualCV (www .visualcv.com) and Resume.com (www.resume.com)—where you can create a résumé online and download it to your computer. If you're not sure you can do a good job, though, don't hesitate to seek help or even hire someone to do it for you. Your school may have a job center or writing lab where students help other students create things like résumés and cover letters.

Whoever does it and however they do it, the final product should be simple and clear. Don't get caught up in choosing fancy typefaces, elaborate graphics or color schemes, funky staggered paragraphs, or other design elements. These things might make you stand out—but quite possibly for the wrong reason. And they will suck up your time and put your focus on the wrong things. Think about what the people who will be reading your résumé want. They want to, above all, save time. They don't want to be looking through résumés. It's not a fun job. It gets old very quickly. It tends to cause headaches. Make their job as easy and quick as possible when they get to yours—they'll appreciate it.

As you can see in her résumé, Sofia uses just one typeface throughout, with only a little bold and italic formatting. Most of the information is in bullet form. Bullets are easy to see and digest. They get right to the point. There are no long sentences to untangle or figure out. You can look at Sofia's résumé and see that nothing is unclear or hard to understand or find. The eye doesn't get stuck anywhere. A reader can grasp the whole thing in a few seconds.

That's not to say your résumé should look exactly like Sofia's. It's a little sparse, to be honest. There's room for Sofia to add a few more things and fill it out a little more. And you can use some creativity and imagination, of course, but don't stray too far from the idea of simplicity. You're not applying to become a graphic designer, after all. The résumé reader has seen dozens of different typefaces, sizes, and fonts in dozens of different arrangements this week alone and is not going to be impressed by such things. Quite the opposite, in fact.

Here are some final things to keep in mind when creating your résumé:

- Proofread it. Then proofread it again. Have three friends or family members proofread it and provide feedback. Have someone at your school's job center or writing lab proofread it and provide feedback. Then proofread their proofread.
- Save it in a few different formats so it is ready to go at any time. Most of the time you'll be uploading the résumé online to companies, and the most commonly requested file formats are Microsoft Word, PDF, and plain text.
- Have several dozen all printed out and ready to give out at a moment's notice.
- Use a variety of active verbs. Highly specific verbs make for better reading. Go through your résumé and highlight all the verbs. How many are repeated? How many are the same old lazy words everybody reaches for every time? See if you can increase the number of different verbs in your résumé.
- Create customized versions for the employers you're really interested in. If you're sending out twenty résumés, but five of them are going to places where you'd be especially excited to work, create a special résumé for each one of those five. Carefully study what kind of company each one is, what skills and experience they say they are looking for, and make your résumé reflect your best effort at being what they want.

- Highlight your accomplishments, not just the routine, day-to-day things you did in some past job. If there is anything in your experience that makes you stand out from the crowd, make it prominent. The last thing you want to be is meek or timid on your résumé. It's one of the few chances you have to brag about yourself without looking obnoxious.

TIDYING UP YOUR ONLINE SOCIAL MEDIA PRESENCE

Before you begin applying for jobs, it is crucial to do a thorough review of your online presence through the years to make sure there's nothing inappropriate there. It's natural sometimes to blow off steam on social media—to rant and complain about people, politicians, or companies, or use colorful language to express yourself in moments of joy or frustration. And it may be okay for friends and family to chuckle at a picture of you drinking a beer or making a rude gesture, but you definitely do not want potential employers seeing stuff like that. It can seriously damage your career prospects.

You need to step back and take a serious look at your online life. Go through and delete or hide anything that could remotely been seen as offensive, crude, immature, or otherwise unprofessional. It should go without saying there should be no references to any illegal activity. Think hard about whether you want potential employers knowing your every political opinion, which may well be the opposite of their own. This house cleaning should include at a minimum Facebook, Twitter, Instagram, LinkedIn, Tumblr, Google+, and any other social media presence you have. Also think about whether you have commented on public websites using your real name.

Bear in mind that this advice holds true whether or not you include links to your social media accounts on your résumé. Interested employers can—and will—enter your name on search engines and click on what pops up. In fact, you should do that too—just in case there is something online you may have forgotten.

Writing Your Cover Letter

So now you have a résumé ready to go. Do you just stick it in an envelope addressed to an employer and pop it in the mail? If only it were that easy. A cover letter is a short message to the employer introducing yourself, summarizing your qualifications, and explaining why you are right for the job. It represents your chance to personalize your application for the job and to look professional.

As with your résumé, you have a little room to be creative with a cover letter, but it should contain the following parts in order, from top to bottom:

- Your name, address, phone number, and e-mail address
- Today's date
- The recipient's name, title, company name, and company address
- Salutation
- Body (usually one to three paragraphs)
- Closing (your signature and name)

Sofia Lynch
99 Saturn Avenue
Turtle Creek, KY 42048
555-321-4321

January 1, 2019

Bob Wilcox
Master Electrician
Wilcox Electric
Bowling Green, KY 42101

Dear Mr. Wilcox,

I am writing to apply for your journeyperson electrician position that I saw advertised in the *Bowling Green Times*. My experience and skills match up very well with your requirements.

You are looking for someone excellent at diagnostics and troubleshooting, and as a four-year apprentice electrician at Franklin Electric, I have extensive experience in those areas. I am also deeply trained in all NEC and Kentucky safety codes and pride myself on never having had any problems in that regard. I am a licensed apprentice in Kentucky and soon will attain journey-level status.

I like your website's professionalism and that you specialize in commercial and residential installation and repair. Those are also my main areas of expertise and preference. Your ad also mentioned you were looking for someone with customer service skills. I have strong skills in that regard, having dealt with customers in my present position and also in two previous jobs, as you can see from my attached resume.

I would very much like to discuss the position further with you at your convenience. I look forward to hearing from you.

Regards,

Sofia Lynch

Sofia Lynch

Example cover letter.

Your cover letter should be as short as possible while still conveying a sense of who you are, what skills you have, and why you want this particular job or to work for this particular company. Do your research into the company and include some details about it in your letter—this demonstrates that you cared enough to take the time to learn something about the company and the job.

Always try to find out the name and title of the person who will be handling your application. This is usually listed in the job posting, but if it is not, taking the time to track it down yourself on the company website can pay off. Think about it: Imagine that you've just read nine cover letters addressed "Dear sir or madam" and then you get a tenth addressed to you using your name. Wouldn't that one catch your attention?

Here are a few more things to keep in mind when writing your cover letter:

- As with the résumé, proofread it many times and have others proofread it, too. You don't want a potential employer to discard the great letter you worked so hard to write just because you forgot to finish a sentence or made some clumsy mistake.
- Use "Mr." for male names and "Ms." for female names in your salutation. If you can't figure out the gender of the person who will be handling your application, just use the full name ("Dear Jamie Smith").
- As much as possible, connect the specific qualifications the company is looking for with your skill set and experience. If they say they are looking for someone with experience fixing Acme discombobulators, they really mean it—everything in the job posting was carefully chosen and put there on purpose, not to fill space. The closer you can make yourself resemble the ideal candidate described in the ad, the more likely the company will call you for an interview.
- If you're lacking one or more qualifications the employer is looking for, just ignore it. Don't call attention to it by pointing it out or making an excuse. Leave it up to them to decide how important it is and whether they still want to call you in for an interview. Your other skills and experience may more than make up for any one deficit.

- You want to seem eager, competent, helpful, and dependable. Think about things from the employer's point of view. Focus your letter much more on what you can do for them than on what they can do for you. Be someone that you would want to hire.
- For more advice on cover letters, check out the free guide by Resume Genius at https://resumegenius.com/cover-letters-the-how-to-guide.

RÉSUMÉS, COVER LETTERS, AND ONLINE JOB APPLICATIONS

Résumés and cover letters are holdovers from the era before the internet—even from before personal computers. They were designed to be typed on paper and delivered through the mail. Obviously these days much of the job application process has moved online. Nevertheless, the essential concepts communicated by the résumé and cover letter haven't changed. Most employers who accept online applications ask that you either e-mail or upload your résumé.

Those who ask you to e-mail your résumé will specify which document formats they accept. PDF format is often preferred, because many programs can display a PDF (including web browsers), and documents in this format are mostly uneditable—that is, they can't easily be changed. In these cases, you attach the résumé to your e-mail, and your e-mail itself becomes the cover letter. The same principles of the cover letter discussed in this section apply to this e-mail, except you skip the addresses and date at the top and begin directly with the salutation.

Some employers direct you to a section on their website where you can upload your résumé. In these cases, it may not be obvious where your cover letter content should go. Look for a text box labeled something like "Personal Statement" or "Additional Information." Those are good places to add whatever you would normally write in a cover letter. If there doesn't seem to be anything like that, see if there is an e-mail link to the hiring manager or the person who will be reading your résumé. Go ahead and send your cover e-mail to this address, mentioning that you have uploaded your résumé (again omitting the addresses and date at the top of your cover letter). Try to use the person's name if it has been given.

The goal of spending so much time and effort crafting a great résumé and cover letter is to achieve one thing: an interview. It's the interview that will determine whether you get the job or not.

Developing Your Interviewing Skills

Sooner or later, your job search will result in what you've been hoping for (or perhaps dreading): a phone call or e-mail requesting that you appear for an interview. When you get that call or e-mail, it means the company is interested in you and is considering hiring you.

Let's back up for a second. An interview is an in-person meeting with someone at the company you're applying for a job with to determine whether you would be a good fit there. It's during the interview that both you and your potential employer will find out whether your expectations about the job—type of work environment, amount of work, hours, type of work, and pay rate—are in line with the company's expectations of you. The interview might be with one person or with more than one person at the same time. You might sit down and talk with one person and then go talk to someone else, and maybe someone else. You might get called back to come in for a second interview on another day. Every company conducts the interview process a little bit differently.

There are lots of books full of endless advice about how to interview—what to say, what not to say, how to dress, how to sit, what to do with your hands, how to arrange your face, how to shake hands, how to cross your legs (or not), and so on. A lot of it may or may not be good advice, but the fact is, by now you pretty much just are who you are. If the company hires you, the person who will be showing up for work everyday is going to be . . . you. So logically, it's in both your and the company's best interest to just be yourself during the interview. You owe that to them and to yourself.

Of course, you want to be your *best* self. Be on your best behavior. But don't worry too much about remembering this or that list of things to do or avoid. You'll be more comfortable if you act naturally. That said, you do want to get the job, and being your best self means a few things:

- Be on time. In fact, try to be five minutes early.
- Look good. Be freshened up and dressed appropriately. (See the next section for more about this.)
- Don't show up hungry or thirsty or having to go to the bathroom. Give yourself plenty of time to take care of those things before you arrive.

Bring a notebook and a pen to the interview. That way you can take some notes, and they'll give you something to do with your hands.

It's a good idea to practice interviewing with a friend or relative. At the very least, you should practice by yourself, answering common interview questions. The Balance Careers offers a long list of common questions asked in interviews at www.thebalancecareers.com/job-interview-questions-and-answers-2061204. You could spend quite a while going through those questions and coming up with answers to prepare yourself.

Come prepared with questions of your own. As soon as you found out about the interview you should have started researching the company, beginning with the company's website. Write down the questions you couldn't answer during your research, and think of anything else you'd like to know. Feel free to ask the interviewer about his or her experience at the company.

When you're talking to the interviewer, relax. Take your time. Use as much detail as you can when describing your education and experience. Look the interviewer in the eye when you talk.

If you know someone who already works at the company, ask him or her for some inside advice and find out whether it's okay to mention his or her name during the interview. If the interviewer finds out you know someone who works there, that can really work in your favor.

DRESSING APPROPRIATELY

A job interview means you have to wear a suit and tie, right? Well, if you want to become a bond trader or a lawyer, yes. But not if you're interviewing for a job in the trade careers. A plumbing company manager would look at you funny if you showed up dressed to the nines.

What you're looking for here is business casual. This is less formal than business attire (like a suit), but a step up from jeans, a T-shirt, and sneakers:

- *For men:* You can't go wrong with khaki pants, a polo or button-up shirt, and brown or black shoes.

- *For women:* Wear nice slacks, a shirt or blouse that isn't too revealing, and nice flats or shoes with a heel that's not too high.

You may want to find out in advance whether the company has a dress code. Don't hesitate to ask the person who's going to interview you if you're unsure what to wear. You can also call the main number and ask the receptionist what people typically wear to interviews.

Once on the job, depending on the line of work, the company may require you to wear a uniform, especially if you'll be interacting with customers and the public. This is something you can ask about during your interview.

Knowing What Employers Expect

You're almost certainly not the only candidate the employer is interviewing for the position. And if you think about it, they would only have called in people who were qualified for the job. That means that, based on education, skills, and experience, all the people who are also interviewing could technically do the job. How, then, will the employer choose from all the candidates?

According to *Forbes* magazine, employers are looking for twelve qualities in you as an employee, and the interview process is meant to bring out these qualities for evaluation.[2] The employer wants to see that you:

- Understand your path
- Know what you want in your career
- Can point to your successes
- Know your strengths
- Think independently
- Like to problem-solve
- Have ambition
- Are proactive
- Like learning new things
- Are goal-oriented
- Work well on a team
- Are responsible

Employers expect that you're not lost and flailing career-wise—that you're not just looking for any old job. They want you to have already examined your own personality and skills and formed an idea of what you want to do and where you want to go. You don't have to know every detail, of course, but they're looking for people with a sense of direction who have made deliberate choices toward a career goal. If your goal is to someday own your own company, by all means, say that. That's impressive. They're looking for impressive people.

Employers also want employees who will stand up for themselves, who aren't afraid to take credit when it's deserved, and who know what they are good at. Despite what you may have thought the workplace would be like, they're not looking for pushovers who are easily bossed around and who automatically do everything they're told without comment or question. Businesses—the ones that want to survive, anyway—should be flexible and nimble and willing to try new things and improve methods and processes to stay ahead of competitors. The only way they can do that in the long term is by hiring people who are like that. People like you. So don't be afraid to express your own opinions and ideas about how you do things in the workplace. Employers *want* that, because over time it helps them grow and get better at what they do.

> "The old saying applies in this field: The more I know, the more I realize how little I know."—Chris Rodriguez, electrician

In just about any field, not just the skilled trades, it's a rare workday where things run smoothly and predictably. Much more often, things go wrong and unforeseen problems crop up, usually at the worst possible times. That's just the way the world works. Employers are looking for workers who understand this, who can think on their feet, and who aren't afraid to roll up their sleeves, dive into new problems, and fix them on their own. If you go to your boss and ask what to do every time something unpredictable or difficult happens, it's only a matter of time before you're actually making your boss's job harder, not easier. After all, your boss is also probably busy trying to solve other problems.

Always aim to make your boss's job easier, not harder. Keeping this simple concept in mind can take you a very long way in the business world.

Every year, innovations in technology and business hit the workplace, throwing everyone a little off track and causing some amount of scrambling to deal with new processes, machinery, systems, and so on. These technological disruptions are just a fact of the modern workplace, and they only seem to be increasing. Unfortunately, what you learn on your first day may not still be the way things are done even six months later. For some people, dealing with constant change becomes a big problem. They get more and more frustrated, sullen, defiant, disgruntled, and loud in their complaints. Employers don't want those people. It's much better for them to find employees who actually like to roll with the punches and learn new things.

Being able to convince an employer that you love to learn new things is one of the best ways to turn yourself into a candidate they won't be able to pass up.

In chapter 2, you learned about the importance of planning. Planning is not just important for succeeding in finding a job—it's important for succeeding in just about everything. Employers want people who understand this, who realize that forming, working toward, and achieving goals is a proven way to get things done. So speak up about your future, about the future of the company, about how you're all going to get from point A to point B. The future of the company depends on employees who are good at setting and achieving goals.

Some interviewers ask a version of a question like, "Can you tell me about one of your failures or when you made a mistake? What happened and what did you do?" This is *not* a trick question. They're not trying to get you to admit something bad so they can use it as an excuse to reject you for not being good enough. The truth is, *everybody* messes up. Even the interviewer asking this question messes up. It's normal. Sometimes messing up is the best or even the *only* way to learn. What they really want to know is how you'll handle yourself when it happens. That's the important thing. Do you blame others, such as team members or customers? Or do you take responsibility for your failures, own up and accept blame, and learn from your mistakes?

One last piece of advice, and in the end this may be the most valuable and crucial of all: Be the kind of person other people like working with. It's sort of the Golden Rule as applied to the workplace.

Following Up

Once you've done some interviews, it's all too easy to just kick back with your phone by you on the sofa and wait for them to call with the good news. Sorry to say, that's not quite good enough. Following up means taking the initiative to contact the interviewer or the person at the company you've been corresponding with to check on the progress of your application.

Following up is a delicate procedure that must be handled with a certain amount of thought and care. A good way to think of it is that you want to be on the interviewer's mind but not in his or her face. You don't want to let too many days go by without any communication, but you also don't want to become annoying.

Following up usually takes place over the phone or through e-mail. You want to follow up after these events (unless they contact you first):

- *After sending a résumé/cover letter to a prospective employer:* If you promptly receive an e-mail or phone call acknowledging your correspondence, that's probably good enough for now. You contacted them, and they contacted you to acknowledge it. You're even, and at that point you should give them around a week to contact you again. If they don't within a week, it's appropriate to contact them again (via the same method, phone or e-mail) to inquire about setting up a time to meet to discuss the matter further. This shows you are still interested.
- *After submitting your application:* If you submitted a job application online, you will likely receive a confirmation e-mail right away. If you mailed in your application, you may get a postcard a few days later to acknowledge it—or you may not. In either case, online or through the mail, if you hear nothing for a week, it's generally okay to contact the company again to inquire about it. This shows you're eager for the job.
- *After being invited to an interview:* A quick, short e-mail to thank them for scheduling an interview is appropriate. This is simply to be polite.

- *After an interview:* Immediately after your interview, you *must* go home and compose an e-mail to your interviewer(s) or to the contact at the company who set up the interview (or both—use your own judgment about what is appropriate). Do this as soon as possible, within the hour if you can. In this e-mail you should thank them for their time and for the opportunity to discuss the position. Say you enjoyed meeting them and look forward to talking again. This is also a matter of politeness, and it shows professionalism, respect, and courtesy.

Always read the instructions carefully regarding submitting an application or corresponding with a company. If they spell out rules for contacting them, do not break those rules without a very good reason. Wondering about how they liked your résumé or when you'll be interviewed are not good enough reasons. The only good reason would be that you are no longer interested or available as a candidate (for example, because you just accepted another job).

THE IMPORTANCE OF FOLLOWING UP

Following up is important for a few reasons. First, you want them to know you're excited and energized about the possibility of working there. Not everyone who is interviewed will follow up. Those who do will naturally appear a little more on the ball and enthusiastic. Second, it could be that they really have forgotten to get back to you. They may have pushed the hiring process to the back burner for a week or two. Contacting them will remind them of their responsibilty to follow through on completing the hire. Finally, following up shows that you have initiative and drive, that you're willing to pick up the phone or send an e-mail to directly address an issue with another person. That itself is a skill and a trait that employers are looking for.

All that said, remember to avoid becoming irritating. Once you follow up, even if you have to leave a voicemail, let it rest. You did your part. Now it's time to be patient. That's not always easy, but keep in mind that they really are busy people. Making hiring decisions isn't easy. Sometimes several people at the company have to get involved to make it happen. It may take them a week or two (sometimes even longer) to contact you after your interview. When they do, it's often to invite you to a second interview.

A second interview is a good sign. It means you're either their first choice and they want to be sure (second interviews are usually with someone else at the company), or you're in the final small group of candidates and they want to compare you all once again. Your strategy in a second interview is essentially the same as in the first interview (see the earlier section "Developing Your Interviewing Skills").

One difference between a first and second interview is that a lot of your questions have now been answered, so you may need to dig a little deeper in terms of what to ask them. They may ask you different questions this time, too, so reviewing the interviewing questions at the link in the previous section is a good idea.

Another difference is that you have slightly higher status now. The first time around, you had no idea whether they would like you or think you were ready for the job. Now you know both things are probably true. This should make you more relaxed, and that's good news for you. As in the first interview, the most important thing is to be yourself—don't put on a false persona or pretend to be someone you're not. That will only end up disappointing everyone once you're on the job.

TALKING ABOUT MONEY AND BENEFITS

The second (or third—yes, there are such things) interview is often where concrete, practical things like benefits and wages are discussed. Be careful! You may be held to whatever you say out loud about these things. It's awfully hard to come back from. If they throw out a per-hour pay rate that's lower than you expected, and you hear yourself saying, "That's fine" . . . well, that's pretty much it. If you end up taking the job, you can bet that's how much you'll be paid.

Sometimes an employer will unexpectedly offer you the job without ever having discussed how much they're willing to pay you. Why would they do that? Well, you may be so excited to get the job offer (you're already imagining calling your mother or boyfriend or girlfriend with the news) that you'll temporarily be willing to accept almost anything—and, of course, that plays to their advantage.

Make no mistake: The employer wants to pay you as little as possible, especially to start with. After all, your starting pay rate will be the basis for your pay rate *forever*. Any raises you ever get—no matter how long your career with the company lasts, and even if you end up being the head honcho—will be calculated based on a percentage of whatever you're currently making, which is based, if you follow the math backward, on your starting salary.

Let's look at an example. Say you get a job offer and they say they're sorry but at this time they can only offer $15 an hour to start, but that you'll be reviewed and eligible for "generous" raises every year once you've proven yourself. Let's also say they offered the same thing to the person they hired before you, but instead of saying okay, he convinced them he was worth $17.50 an hour and was willing to stand by that amount for several days as they went back and forth, until they finally agreed. Let's compare the two of you:

$15.00 × 40 hours = $600 per week × 52 = $31,200 annually
$17.50 × 40 hours = $700 per week × 52 = $36,400 annually

That's a difference of $5,200 in just the first year. Even if the two of you never got a raise at all, after ten years the difference would add up to $52,000, and after twenty years the gap would be $104,000! But let's say you both got raises and promotions over the years—some big, some small, but averaging a conservative 3 percent per year. Table 4.1 shows how this difference would add up (with all numbers rounded to the nearest dollar).

Your coworker would end up making $139,677 more than you would over twenty years. In many places, that's enough to buy a nice house. Another way to think of it is that, at some point in your sixth year working for the company together, your coworker would have made *your entire annual starting salary more than you had*. In other words, it would have been better at that point for you to hold out for that extra $2.50 an hour *for a whole year* than to take the job at $15 an hour.

Talking about money isn't easy, and the fact that it makes many people uncomfortable is often an advantage to the employer. Hopefully by now you can see what a huge difference it makes to start a job at even a slightly higher pay rate. Don't be afraid to negotiate for even a little bit more money to start with. The worst they will say is no.

Table 4.1. Comparison of 3 Percent Raises on Wages over Twenty Years

Year	$15 Starting Wage	$17.50 Starting Wage	Difference
1	$31,200	$36,400	$5,200
2	$32,136	$37,492	$5,356
3	$33,100	$38,616	$5,516
4	$34,093	$39,774	$5,681
5	$35,115	$40,967	$5,852
6	$36,168	$42,196	$6,028
7	$37,253	$43,461	$6,208
8	$38,370	$44,764	$6,394
9	$39,521	$46,106	$6,585
10	$40,706	$47,489	$6,783
11	$41,927	$48,913	$6,986
12	$43,184	$50,380	$7,196
13	$44,479	$51,891	$7,412
14	$45,813	$53,447	$7,634
15	$47,187	$55,050	$7,863
16	$48,602	$56,701	$8,099
17	$50,060	$58,402	$8,324
18	$51,561	$60,154	$8,593
19	$53,107	$61,958	$8,851
20	$54,700	$63,816	$9,116
Total	$838,282	$977,977	$139,677

A few tips on negotiation:

- It's better to not be the first one to state a number. You want them to say it first, because whatever you say, their goal will be to talk you down from that. Or—maybe even worse—they'll accept your number. If that happens, you know for a fact that you could have suggested a higher number, but now you can't.
- One thing employers commonly say is that the starting wage is fixed, that their hands are tied, that there's nothing they can do, that you have

to take it or leave it. They say this because 90 percent of people will end up taking it—and you saw in table 4.1 just how much money the company can save that way. But don't believe them. Pay is always negotiable, no matter what. If they want you, and you stick to your guns, don't be surprised if they agree to your number or offer you a compromise number you can live with.

- Don't worry that an employer will be offended if you ask for more money, or that they'll think you're just greedy and won't want to hire you anymore. It's a law of economics that people want to maximize a transaction to their benefit. Asking for more money is an economically rational thing for you to do. They understand—after all, they're playing the exact same game in reverse. Are they worried that *you'll* be offended by *their* low offer? No, they're not.

- If you know you're their best candidate and it's clear that they want to hire you, that tells you two things: (1) If this company wants to hire you, other companies will also want to hire you, and (2) you now have a certain amount of power. Think about how much time and energy they've already spent getting to this point with you. If you walk away, they'll have to either start the whole process over or turn to their next-best choice. They don't want to do either of those things. The more patience you can muster—the more willing you are to let a day or two or three go by without caving in to their lowball offer—the more power you have, and the more likely they will accept your number.

- If they turn out to be even more stubborn than you—and you still want the job—before you back down and accept their offer, consider asking for better benefits (if they offer benefits). An extra week of vacation time, the top-tier health insurance plan for the price of the lower-tier one, or eyesight or dental coverage are examples of reasonable things to ask for. Sometimes benefits are easier to haggle over than pay.

The fine art of negotiating pay and benefits is well beyond the scope of this book. Many smart people have written a whole lot about the subject. The Muse article "How to Negotiate Salary" is a good place to start if you want to learn more about how to do it well.[3]

FROM AIR FORCE TO ELECTRICIAN

Chris Rodriguez.
*Courtesy of
Chris Rodriguez*

Chris Rodriguez is an electrician in Atlanta, Georgia. He joined the air force when he was eighteen. When it came time to choose an occupation within the service, his mother suggested electrician. He is still excited by his work as an electrician, although he tends to be a bit of a workaholic.

Why did you choose to become an electrician?

When I joined the air force. I wanted to jump out of planes and do something dangerous at the time, like most kids do, but it was the first time in my life that I actually listened to my mother. Always listen to your mother. I was on the phone with her while I was on a cigarette break in basic training. I read her my list of jobs that the air force was offering me, and electrician was on there. She told me to take that one, that they get paid "good money" and that I would have something to fall back on when I got out. I listened to her, and here I am almost thirty years later still happy that I did.

I was in the air force for ten and a half years, and I ended up getting medically retired from it. I was a musician throughout the 1990s and most of the 2000s. Not on the world stage or anything like that, although I was at that level. The music industry is a very fickle and ugly world that I left behind in order to do something a little more stable that had more opportunity and longevity. My midlife crisis was not that of the typical male. I wanted to settle down, get a wife, maybe have some kids, drive a normal vehicle, buy a house, own a charcoal grill, and pass out Halloween candy every year. I had the greatest wild and insane years that one could have, but for the past eight years my life has been exactly that: normal. I'm excited by work, although I tend to be a bit of a workaholic. My record is forty-eight straight working days in a row. That included weekends, two holidays, and my birthday.

What is a typical day on the job for you?

A typical day for my job starts with knowing the name of the customer's house or business that I will be working at that day. I have on my uniform, swing through the Starbucks drive-through, then head to my calls. Typically I schedule one to two calls a day. Once there, the customer will tell me what they need done, I perform the work they need, and if there is anything else I see that should be addressed for safety reasons, I inform them. Once I'm done with that job, I either head to the next call, if I have one scheduled, or I go home. A typical call is installing electrical outlets, running wires, hanging ceiling fans, installing recessed lighting, or trouble-shooting electrical equipment or circuitry that doesn't work properly.

What's the best part of your job?

I am lucky enough to have started my own company, so far and away the best part about my job is that I don't answer to anyone. I don't have someone calling me to find out my status or making demands on my time. I work when I want to, and I take time off when I want to. Other than that, the job is a lot of fun. I do the same job over and over, only in a different environment every day. I'm not chained to a desk in an office. I get to meet new and exciting people almost every day. I do electrical service work, which means that customers mainly call me directly. I deal with everyone from normal everyday people to athletes, musicians, homemakers, and politicians. I take breaks whenever I want, which is only rarely. My job doesn't really require structured break times or lunches. I tend to not take them because my interest is in getting the job done as quickly as possible so I can get back to my private life.

What's the worst or most challenging part of your job?

There is very little dependable help. The hardest part of the job is that we have very little human interaction once the selling part is over. We're constantly driving all over the city to our calls, but that's about it. The worst part of the job is that time waits for nobody. Your body will eventually start wearing down. It can be physically demanding at times. The older I get, the harder it is to do the same things I used to do. Crawling in basements or climbing through attics tends to get increasingly difficult as the years pass. It's not enough to really slow me down yet, but it does let me know that there is an expiration date attached to this body. So I try to keep in moderately good shape. Arthritis is something that will creep in eventually. Hand soreness and tightness is inescapable after nearly thirty years in the trade. It does get lonely working for yourself, so you end up either calling your friends on the phone a lot or listening to a lot of music.

What's the most surprising thing about your job?

How much it pays. It's ridiculously profitable. Most people have no idea. The ones who do have an idea are those who have had to pay a good electrician. I came home from the military and was going to attend engineering school. Once I found out about the electrical service industry, I left that engineering idea far behind.

What's next? Where do you see yourself going from here?

Next thing for me is to hire other capable electricians and have them go out and perform the work that is needed. Most electricians despise the customer interaction and the sales aspects of service work. Most just want to come to work, do their job, and clock out at the end of the day. The sales industry is all commission based, and that terrifies most people. Each week, you start out with a zero paycheck. So my next move is to start expanding and hiring about five electricians [who] are able to perform the work at the levels that I require. I'm a master electrician, and my customers expect that level of craftsmanship, so my guys need to be at that level. I can sell jobs well into my seventies, so sales is the direction I'm headed in. I will either hire people who can sell and install by themselves, or I'll hire people who can do the installation work but who just aren't able to sell it due to the stress of that lifestyle. I have several far larger company visions that I hope to expand into once those workers are in place. Hopefully, I can build this company into a far larger service corporation with a national and potentially global scope. But way before that I'll be adding more technicians in the current market.

Did your education prepare you for the job?

Absolutely. I do mathematics daily, algebra daily. Hundreds of calculations and formulas have to be understood in order to pass the state license examination. High school helped, the limited college that I attended helped a very small amount, and my technical schooling in the military helped me out immensely. I've met other electricians who don't have a formal education in this field, and they operate on memory of what they learned versus understanding what it is that they're doing. This is a career choice, like others, in which it's impossible to know everything. The old saying applies in this field: The more I know, the more I realize how little I know.

Is the job what you expected?

Not at all. I never knew this career would be this enjoyable. I definitely had no idea it would be this profitable.

Summary

This chapter covered writing your résumé and cover letter, applying for jobs through the mail and online, polishing your interviewing skills, and getting down to brass tacks with regard to money. You learned the vital importance of communication, both written and verbal, to a successful job search. And you discovered tips and tricks that should serve you long into your career.

You've come to the end of the main part of the book. Hopefully, by now you have a good sense of what it takes to pursue a career in these particular skilled trades. You've picked a solid, well-established career path that has a proud history and a bright future. Best of luck in your career endeavors!

Glossary

apprenticeship: A period of two to five years during which a new employee undergoes an earn-while-you-learn program under expert supervision to learn the details of a particular trade. Completion of an apprenticeship usually results in elevation to journeyman status and the ability to work the trade independently.

artificial intelligence (AI): The increasing use of machines to supplement or replace human analysis and decision making.

associate's degree: A two-year academic degree with concentrated coursework in a particular field.

automation: The replacement of human labor by machines, such as factory robots and grocery store self-checkouts.

Automotive Service Excellence (ASE): The National Institute for Automotive Service Excellence is an independent nonprofit organization that promotes high standards and quality service among auto service techs and mechanics. ASE certification requires two years of on-the-job training or one year of on-the-job-training and a two-year associate's degree in automotive repair, and passing the ASE certification test.

career and technical education (CTE): Curricula in many high schools, similar to what used to be called shop classes, offering classes in automotive technology, building technology, drafting and mechanical design, business technology, and computer technology.

certificate: A credential awarded upon completion of training by certain vocational schools.

certification: A credential issued by a recognized authority such as a school, organization or association, or government office that affirms completion of certain requirements.

community college: A public postsecondary educational institution offering career and vocational courses and programs leading to a diploma, certificate, or associate's degree.

contractor: A construction company that bids on and completes construction, repair, or renovation projects. Also refers to a representative of such a company, especially the owner.

craftsperson: A skilled specialist in a construction trade, such as carpenter, mason, or machine operator.

degree: A credential awarded on completion of a two-year associate's or four-year bachelor's degree program.

diploma: A credential awarded upon completion of training by certain vocational schools.

economics: The study of how people, organizations, companies, and governments conduct transactions and interact in markets.

Environmental Protection Agency (EPA): A federal government agency charged with regulating things that impact the environment. HVAC technicians and auto mechanics who work on vehicle air-conditioning systems must pass an EPA test in order to be licensed to handle certain chemicals, such as refrigerants.

Free Application for Federal Student Aid (FAFSA): An application that current and prospective students submit to determine eligibility for postsecondary student financial aid.

General Educational Development (GED): An exam that confers a credential that is the equivalent of a high school diploma, which you can use to qualify for jobs.

journeyman: A midlevel practitioner of a trade, such as a plumber or electrician, who has completed an apprenticeship. Journeymen have a few years of experience and can work independently without supervision. They usually must pass a state exam to rise to this status. After journeyman comes master level.

heating, ventilation, and cooling (HVAC): A field in the skilled trades involving work on heating and cooling systems, ventilation systems, and sometimes refrigeration equipment.

lineman: An electrician who works outdoors on power lines and other utility equipment.

master: A top-level practitioner of a trade, such as master plumber or master electrician, who has gone beyond journeyman status and, in many cases, passed a state exam. Masters have many years of experience and are paid at the highest level.

National Electrical Code (NEC): A set of safety standards and guidelines for electrical wiring and equipment. An updated NEC is published every few years by the National Fire Protection Association.

on-the-job training: An arrangement, such as in an apprenticeship, in which a new employee is paid a starting wage to learn from an experienced worker who guides and directs the training.

pipefitter: A professional similar to plumber, who works with pipes that carry various kinds of materials, including high-pressure gases.

postsecondary education: Any formal coursework done after high school, such as at a college, university, junior college, community college, or vocational or technical school.

skilled trade: Any of a group of occupations involving the installation, maintenance, and repair of machinery, equipment, systems, and components of building construction—for example, electrician, HVAC technician, plumber, automotive service technician, and construction laborer.

social networking: Using the connections and affiliations between people and groups of people you know in order to build and expand your contacts.

union: An organization of workers in a particular field or group of fields that represents workers at the bargaining table with management. Unions negotiate how companies should allocate and distribute their profits, making sure workers receive their fair share and aren't left out.

voice-data-video (VDV): A low-voltage electrical system.

vocational school: A postsecondary educational institution dedicated to focused technical training and development of hands-on skills in various skilled trades and other technical fields.

wireman: An electrician who works indoors on wiring in buildings.

Notes

Introduction: So You Want a Career
in the Skilled Trades?

1. Monster.com, "Skilled Trades Careers," www.monster.com/skilled-trades -careers.

2. Bureau of Labor Statistics, US Department of Labor, "Installation, Maintenance, and Repair Occupations," www.bls.gov/oes/current/oes_stru.htm#49 -0000.

3. Also sometimes "heating, ventilation, and cooling." Sometimes an *R*, for "re-frigeration," is added, so it becomes HVACR. For simplicity, this book uses HVAC.

4. Joshua Wright, "America's Skilled Trades Dilemma: Shortages Loom as Most In-Demand Group of Workers Ages," *Forbes*, March 7, 2013, www.forbes.com/ sites/emsi/2013/03/07/americas-skilled-trades-dilemma-shortages-loom-as-most-in -demand-group-of-workers-ages/ - 36ee0e076397.

Chapter 1

1. Salary.com, "Salary for Electrician II in the United States," https://www1 .salary.com/Electrician-II-Salary.html.

2. Salary.com, "Salary for Aircraft Electrician in the United States," https:// www1.salary.com/Aircraft-Electrician-Salary.html.

3. Bureau of Labor Statistics, US Department of Labor, "Union Members Summary," www.bls.gov/news.release/union2.nr0.htm.

4. Daniel Browning, "Are Skilled Trade Jobs Safe in the Age of Automation?" *The NEWS*, August 3, 2018, www.achrnews.com/blogs/16-guest-blog/post/139512-are -skilled-trade-jobs-safe-in-the-age-of-automation.

5. Bureau of Labor Statistics, US Department of Labor, "Electricians: Job Outlook," www.bls.gov/ooh/construction-and-extraction/electricians.htm#tab-6.

6. Bureau of Labor Statistics, US Department of Labor, "Electricians: Job Outlook," www.bls.gov/ooh/construction-and-extraction/electricians.htm#tab-6.

7. Bureau of Labor Statistics, US Department of Labor, "Heating, Air Conditioning, and Refrigeration Mechanics and Installers," www.bls.gov/ooh/instal lation-maintenance-and-repair/heating-air-conditioning-and-refrigeration-mechanics -and-installers.htm.

8. Bureau of Labor Statistics, US Department of Labor, "Plumbers, Pipefitters, and Steamfitters," www.bls.gov/ooh/construction-and-extraction/plumbers-pipefitters -and-steamfitters.htm.

9. Bureau of Labor Statistics, US Department of Labor, "What Construction Laborers and Helpers Do," www.bls.gov/ooh/construction-and-extraction/construc tion-laborers-and-helpers.htm#tab-2.

10. Bureau of Labor Statistics, US Department of Labor, "What Construction Equipment Operators Do," www.bls.gov/ooh/construction-and-extraction/construc tion-equipment-operators.htm#tab-2.

11. Bureau of Labor Statistics, US Department of Labor, "What Construction Managers Do," www.bls.gov/ooh/management/construction-managers.htm#tab-2.

12. Bureau of Labor Statistics, US Department of Labor, "Automotive Service Technicians and Mechanics," www.bls.gov/ooh/installation-maintenance-and-repair/ automotive-service-technicians-and-mechanics.htm.

Chapter 2

1. Bureau of Labor Statistics, US Department of Labor, "How to Become an Electrician," www.bls.gov/ooh/construction-and-extraction/electricians.htm#tab-4.

2. Bureau of Labor Statistics, US Department of Labor, "How to Become a Plumber, Pipefitter, or Steamfitter," www.bls.gov/ooh/construction-and-extraction/ plumbers-pipefitters-and-steamfitters.htm#tab-4.

Chapter 3

1. National Center for Education Statistics, "Number of Degree-Granting Postsecondary Institutions and Enrollment in These Institutions, by Enrollment Size, Contro, and Classification of Insititution: Fall 2016," https://nces.ed.gov/programs/ digest/d17/tables/dt17_317.40.asp.

2. Mark Nowak, "Electrician Schools & Programs," Accredited Schools Online, www.accreditedschoolsonline.org/vocational-trade-school/electrician.

3. College Choice, "Best HVAC Programs," www.collegechoice.net/rankings/best-hvac-programs.

4. Schools.com, "Plumbing Degree Programs," www.schools.com/programs/plumbing.

5. TheBestSchools.org, "The 20 Best Auto Mechanic Schools," https://thebest schools.org/rankings/best-automotive-mechanic-schools.

6. Accredited Schools Online, "Online Vocational Trade Schools & Degrees," www.accreditedschoolsonline.org/vocational-trade-school/online.

7. Dawn Rosenberg McCay, "What Is an Apprenticeship?" The Balance Careers, www.thebalancecareers.com/what-is-an-apprenticeship-526218.

8. United States Department of Labor, "Frequently Asked Questions," www .apprenticeship.gov/faqs.

9. Employment and Training Administration, US Department of Labor, "Apprentices National Growth Chart," https://doleta.gov/oa/data_statistics.cfm.

10. College Board, https://trends.collegeboard.org/sites/default/files/2018-trends -in-college-pricing.pdf.

11. Johanna Sorrentino, "How Much Does Trade School Cost?" Real Work Matters, June 14, 2016, www.rwm.org/articles/how-much-does-trade-school-cost.

Chapter 4

1. The Ladders, "Keeping an Eye on Recruiter Behavior," https://cdn.theladders .net/static/images/basicSite/pdfs/TheLadders-EyeTracking-StudyC2.pdf.

2. Liz Ryan, "12 Qualities Employers Look for When They're Hiring," *Forbes,* March 2, 2016, www.forbes.com/sites/lizryan/2016/03/02/12-qualities-employers -look-for-when-theyre-hiring/#8ba06d22c242.

3. The Muse, "How to Negotiate Salary: 37 Tips You Need to Know," www.the muse.com/advice/how-to-negotiate-salary-37-tips-you-need-to-know.

Resources

*H*ere is a list of online resources you can use to continue your investigation into a career in the skilled trades.

Information on the Skilled Trades

Bureau of Labor Statistics (BLS), www.bls.gov
Career Outlook (from BLS), www.bls.gov/careeroutlook/subject/home.htm
Explore the Trades, https://explorethetrades.org
Monster.com, Skilled Trades Careers, www.monster.com/skilled-trades-careers
Occupational Outlook Handbook (from BLS), www.bls.gov/ooh

Information on Unions

Center for Union Facts, www.unionfacts.com/cuf
Electrical Training Alliance, www.electricaltrainingalliance.org
International Association of Machinists and Aerospace Workers (auto mechanic), www.unionmechanic.org
International Brotherhood of Electrical Workers (electrician), www.ibew.org
Laborers' International Union of North America (construction), www.liuna.org
National Electrical Contractors Association (electrician), www.neca.org
North America's Building Trades Unions (construction), www.nabtu.org
United Association (plumber, HVAC), www.ua.org

Paying for School

Free Application for Federal Student Aid, https://studentaid.ed.gov/sa/fafsa

Grant information, https://studentaid.ed.gov/types/grants-scholarships

Scholarship information, www.gocollege.com/financial-aid/scholarships/types

Student loan information, https://bigfuture.collegeboard.org/pay-for-college/loans/types-of-college-loans

Finding Apprenticeships

Apprenticeship Finder, www.careeronestop.org/Toolkit/Training/find-apprenticeships.aspx

Apprenticeship Sponsor Database (DOL), https://oa.doleta.gov/bat.cfm

Apprenticeships at Department of Labor (DOL), www.apprenticeship.gov

Registered Apprenticeships (DOL), www.dol.gov/featured/apprenticeship/faqs

Finding Vocational Schools

Accredited Schools Online, www.accreditedschoolsonline.org/vocational-trade-school

Choosing a Vocational School (FTC), www.consumer.ftc.gov/articles/0241-choosing-vocational-school

Council for Higher Education Accreditation, www.chea.org/search-institutions

Educations.com Career Test, www.educations.com/career-test

Finding a Reputable School, www.consumer.ftc.gov/articles/0241-choosing-vocational-school

GED Exam, www.ged.com

Princeton Review Online Career Quiz, www.princetonreview.com/quiz/career-quiz

Top Automotive Service/Mechanic Programs, https://thebestschools.org/rankings/best-automotive-mechanic-schools

Top Electrician Programs, www.accreditedschoolsonline.org/vocational-trade-school/electrician

Top HVAC Programs, www.collegechoice.net/rankings/best-hvac-programs

Top Online Programs, www.accreditedschoolsonline.org/vocational-trade-school/online

Top Overall Trade Schools, www.forbes.com/sites/cartercoudriet/2018/08/15/
the-top-25-two-year-trade-schools-colleges-that-can-solve-the-skills-gap
/#3590e1b33478
Top Plumbing Programs, www.schools.com/programs/plumbing
Trade Schools Guide, www.trade-schools.net

Finding Jobs

The Balance Careers, www.balancecareers.com
Craigslist, www.craigslist.org
Indeed.com, www.indeed.com
Monster.com, www.monster.com
The Muse, www.themuse.com
Resume.com, www.resume.com
Resume Genius, www.resumegenius.com
Salary.com, www.salary.com
VisualCV, www.visualcv.com

Certification

Automotive Service Excellence, www.ase.com
Environmental Protection Agency, Section 608, www.epa.gov/section608/section
-608-technician-certification-test-topics
National Electrical Code, www.nfpa.org/codes-and-standards/all-codes-and
-standards/list-of-codes-and-standards/detail?code=70

Bibliography

Accredited Schools Online. "Online Vocational Trade Schools & Degrees." Retrieved October 30, 2018, from www.accreditedschoolsonline.org/vocational-trade-school/online.

Browning, Daniel. "Are Skilled Trade Jobs Safe in the Age of Automation?" *The NEWS*. Retrieved October 30, 2018, from www.achrnews.com/blogs/16-guest-blog/post/139512-are-skilled-trade-jobs-safe-in-the-age-of-automation.

Bureau of Labor Statistics, US Department of Labor. "Automotive Service Technicians and Mechanics." Retrieved October 30, 2018, from www.bls.gov/ooh/installation-maintenance-and-repair/automotive-service-technicians-and-mechanics.htm.

———. "Electricians: Job Outlook." Retrieved October 30, 2018, from www.bls.gov/ooh/construction-and-extraction/electricians.htm#tab-6.

———. "Heating, Air Conditioning, and Refrigeration Mechanics and Installers." Retrieved October 30, 2018, from www.bls.gov/ooh/installation-maintenance-and-repair/heating-air-conditioning-and-refrigeration-mechanics-and-installers.htm.

———. "How to Become an Electrician." Retrieved October 30, 2018, from www.bls.gov/ooh/construction-and-extraction/electricians.htm#tab-4.

———. "How to Become a Plumber, Pipefitter, or Steamfitter." Retrieved October 30, 2018, from www.bls.gov/ooh/construction-and-extraction/plumbers-pipefitters-and-steamfitters.htm#tab-4.

———. "Installation, Maintenance, and Repair Occupations." Retrieved October 30, 2018, from www.bls.gov/oes/current/oes_stru.htm#49-0000.

———. "Plumbers, Pipefitters, and Steamfitters." Retrieved October 30, 2018, from www.bls.gov/ooh/construction-and-extraction/plumbers-pipefitters-and-steamfitters.htm.

———. "Union Members Summary." Retrieved October 30, 2018, from www.bls.gov/news.release/union2.nr0.htm.

———. "What Construction Laborers and Helpers Do." Retrieved October 30, 2018, from www.bls.gov/ooh/construction-and-extraction/construction -laborers-and-helpers.htm#tab-2.

———. "What Construction Equipment Operators Do." Retrieved October 30, 2018, from www.bls.gov/ooh/construction-and-extraction/construction -equipment-operators.htm#tab-2.

———. "What Construction Managers Do." Retrieved October 30, 2018, from www.bls.gov/ooh/management/construction-managers.htm#tab-2.

College Board. Retrieved October 30, 2018, from https://trends.collegeboard .org/sites/default/files/2018-trends-in-college-pricing.pdf.

College Choice. "Best HVAC Programs." Retrieved October 30, 2018, from www.collegechoice.net/rankings/best-hvac-programs.

Employment and Training Administration, US Department of Labor. "Apprentices National Growth Chart." Retrieved October 30, 2018, from https://doleta.gov/oa/data_statistics.cfm.

The Ladders. "Keeping an Eye on Recruiter Behavior." Retrieved October 30, 2018, from https://cdn.theladders.net/static/images/basicSite/pdfs/ TheLadders-EyeTracking-StudyC2.pdf.

McCay, Dawn Rosenberg. "What Is an Apprenticeship?" The Balance Careers. Retrieved October 30, 2018, from www.thebalancecareers.com/ what-is-an-apprenticeship-526218.

Monster.com. "Skilled Trades Careers." Retrieved October 30, 2018, from www.monster.com/skilled-trades-careers.

National Center for Education Statistics. "Number of Degree-Granting Postsecondary Institutions and Enrollment in These Institutions, by Enrollment Size, Control, and Classification of Institution: Fall 2016." Retrieved October 30, 2018, from https://nces.ed.gov/programs/digest/ d17/tables/dt17_317.40.asp.

Nowak, Mark. "Electrician Schools & Programs." Accredited Schools Online. Retrieved October 30, 2018, from www.accreditedschoolsonline.org/ vocational-trade-school/electrician.

Ryan, Liz. "12 Qualities Employers Look for When They're Hiring." *Forbes*, March 2, 2016. Retrieved October 30, 2018, from www.forbes.com/sites/ lizryan/2016/03/02/12-qualities-employers-look-for-when-theyre-hiring/ #8ba06d22c242.

Salary.com. "Salary for Aircraft Electrician in the United States." Retrieved October 30, 2018, from https://www1.salary.com/Aircraft-Electrician -Salary.html.

———. "Salary for Electrician II in the United States." Retrieved October 30, 2018, from https://www1.salary.com/Electrician-II-Salary.html.

Schools.com. "Plumbing Degree Programs." Retrieved October 30, 2018, from www.schools.com/programs/plumbing.

Sorrentino, Johanna. "How Much Does Trade School Cost?" Real Work Matters, June 14, 2016. Retrieved October 30, 2018, from www.rwm.org/ articles/how-much-does-trade-school-cost.

TheBestSchools.org. "The 20 Best Auto Mechanic Schools." Retrieved October 30, 2018, from https://thebestschools.org/rankings/best-auto motive-mechanic-schools.

US Department of Labor, "Frequently Asked Questions." Retrieved October 20, 2018, from www.apprenticeship.gov/faqs.

Wright, Joshua. "America's Skilled Trades Dilemma: Shortages Loom as Most-In-Demand Group of Workers Ages." *Forbes*, March 7, 2013. Retrieved October 30, 2018, from www.forbes.com/sites/emsi/2013/03/07/americas -skilled-trades-dilemma-shortages-loom-as-most-in-demand-group-of -workers-ages/#36ee0e076397.

About the Author

Corbin Collins is a roving writer and editor currently based in Indiana after stints in San Francisco, Ireland, and the Netherlands. He holds two master's degrees in English literature, one from Northwestern University and one from the Iowa Writers' Workshop at the University of Iowa. He has worked on hundreds of books for numerous publishers in his career, spanning topics including computer science, networking, languages, investing, statistics, music, and career advancement. When not engaged in bookmaking, he enjoys playing music with other people and hanging with his family. This is his first book for Rowman & Littlefield.

www.ingramcontent.com/pod-product-compliance
Lightning Source LLC
Chambersburg PA
CBHW030109100325
23067CB00006B/56